STATISTICS DIRECTORATE

CONSTRUCTION PRICE INDICES

Sources and Methods

ORGANISATION FOR ECONOMIC CO-OPERATION AND DEVELOPMENT
STATISTICAL OFFICE OF THE EUROPEAN COMMUNITIES

ORGANISATION FOR ECONOMIC CO-OPERATION AND DEVELOPMENT

Pursuant to Article 1 of the Convention signed in Paris on 14th December 1960, and which came into force on 30th September 1961, the Organisation for Economic Co-operation and Development (OECD) shall promote policies designed:

- to achieve the highest sustainable economic growth and employment and a rising standard of living in Member countries, while maintaining financial stability, and thus to contribute to the development of the world economy;
- to contribute to sound economic expansion in Member as well as non-member countries in the process of economic development; and
- to contribute to the expansion of world trade on a multilateral, non-discriminatory basis in accordance with international obligations.

The original Member countries of the OECD are Austria, Belgium, Canada, Denmark, France, Germany, Greece, Iceland, Ireland, Italy, Luxembourg, the Netherlands, Norway, Portugal, Spain, Sweden, Switzerland, Turkey, the United Kingdom and the United States. The following countries became Members subsequently through accession at the dates indicated hereafter: Japan (28th April 1964), Finland (28th January 1969), Australia (7th June 1971), New Zealand (29th May 1973), Mexico (18th May 1994), the Czech Republic (21st December 1995), Hungary (7th May 1996), Poland (22nd November 1996) and the Republic of Korea (12th December 1996). The Commission of the European Communities takes part in the work of the OECD (Article 13 of the OECD Convention).

Publié en français sous le titre :

INDICES DES PRIX A LA CONSTRUCTION
Sources et méthodes

FOREWORD

This publication is the result of joint work between the Statistics Directorate of the Organisation for Economic Co-operation and Development (OECD) and the Statistical Office of the European Communities (EUROSTAT). The objectives of this collaboration were to outline conceptual problems in the development of construction price indices, based on a comparative description of the methodologies currently used by Member countries of the OECD and the European Union.

Such information will enable national statistical institutes, or other organisations compiling construction price indices, to compare their methodology and data sources with those currently used in other countries. It will also provide a range of options for countries in the process of creating their own indices, or overhauling existing indices. At present there is very little multi-country documentation available on construction price indices.

The level of activity in the construction sector is one of the key determinants of the level of short-term economic activity in Member countries. The demand for reliable construction price indices arises from the need to assess real changes in the output from these activities which cannot be derived solely through reference to regular building and construction statistics. These indices have a wide range of applications including deflation of components of national accounts, adjustment of construction contracts and leases, and as a basis for indexation for insurance purposes.

At the moment, there is considerable variation in the concepts underlying the compilation of construction price indices by Member countries, as well as in the price components and methodologies used. This variation is the result of the different administrative and legislative environment, and differing physical characteristics, such as geographic size, population density, climate, etc. in which organisations undertaking construction activity operate in each country. Another factor are the different uses of the construction indices compiled.

The Statistics Directorate of the OECD and EUROSTAT are greatly indebted to the statistical offices of OECD and European Union Member countries for their co-operation. Without this assistance, it would not have been possible to produce this publication.

This publication is presented on the joint responsibility of the Secretary General of the OECD, and the Director-General of EUROSTAT.

Louis Kincannon
Director
Statistics Directorate
OECD

Yves Franchet
Director-General
EUROSTAT

TABLE OF CONTENTS

TABLE OF CONTENTS (cont.)

TABLE OF CONTENTS (cont.)

ABBREVIATIONS

CPI	Consumer price index
ESA	European System of National and Regional Accounts in the European Community
EUROSTAT	Statistical Office of the European Communities
GDP	Gross domestic product
GFCF	Gross fixed capital formation
ISIC	International Standard Industrial Classification
NACE	Statistical Classification of Economic Activities in the European Community
OECD	Organisation for Economic Co-operation and Development
PPI	Producer price index
SNA	System of National Accounts
VAT	Value added tax

This publication provides an outline of the sources and methods used by OECD and European Union Member countries in the compilation of price indices for construction activity. Its objectives are: to provide information on techniques used on a country by country basis; a conceptual framework for the compilation of construction price indices; and indications of best practice in the compilation of these indices. Such information will enable OECD and European Union Member countries to compare their methodology/data sources with those currently used in other countries. It will also provide a range of options for countries in the process of creating their own indices, or overhauling existing indices. These options may be either adopted in their entirety, or modified according to their own circumstances.

The term construction covers a wide variety of activities, these include the construction of dwellings, non-residential buildings, and civil engineering works such as roads, bridges, dams, etc. Construction activity also encompasses repair, renovations, rehabilitation and maintenance of existing structures, etc.

The diversity of construction activity is the cause of one of the major problems in the compilation of construction price indices, that of comparability. The items comprising an index and their relative weights are the result of different norms and standards that apply in each country. For example, when comparing indices compiled by different countries for housing construction, account needs to be taken of differences in climate, culture, level of affluence, legislative standards, physical characteristics (e.g. geographic size, population density, terrain) etc. These factors even influence what is included in a "house", and therefore the range of items included in a price index of house construction. There is considerable variation between countries in the inclusion/exclusion of items such as land, utility connection, fixtures, transport of materials, architects fees, etc. from their indices.

At present there is very little multi-country documentation available on construction price indices. This publication complements two previous publications produced by the OECD in 1994, *Consumer Price Indices - Sources and Methods*, and *Producer Price Indices - Sources and Methods,* and a publication produced by EUROSTAT in 1995, *Industrial Trends: National Methods.*

In February 1996 EUROSTAT hosted a seminar on construction price indices. Papers from this seminar providing detailed descriptions of methodologies for the compilation of these indices for some European Union countries will be published in *Methodological Aspects of Construction Price Indices* in late 1996.

The demand for price indices for construction activity arises from the need to assess real changes in the output from these activities (i.e. to create a constant value series) which cannot be derived solely through reference to regular building and construction statistics.

Construction price indices are used in guaranteed value clauses in rental, leasing, and other contracts; adjustment of sales contracts for buildings under construction; and as a basis for indexation for insurance purposes. They are also used to deflate national accounts estimates of output of construction activities, and gross fixed capital formation in residential construction.

In summary, construction price indices are used to track changes/trends in the cost (or price) of construction. They do not provide information on the current market value of construction work, earning capacity, or rental values.

This publication comprises three sections.

Section 1 outlines basic concepts and describes the relationship between producer price indices and construction price indices, elements of construction industry prices, the main types of construction indices, and a typology of methods used by OECD and European Union Member countries in their compilation.

Section 2 outlines the major problems involved in compilation of construction price indices, sources of information used, and describes some of the major elements in their compilation. The latter includes construction activity coverage, items in the indices, the calculation of weights, basis of prices, the alternate approaches to price collection, and issues relating to area coverage. Examples of best practice are also provided.

Section 3 briefly describes each of the three main construction price indices compiled in OECD and European Union Member countries. These are: input price indices, output price indices, and seller's price indices. Where appropriate, more detailed descriptions are provided for some countries to illustrate important aspects of a number of the concepts outlined in Section 1, and compilation issues described in Section 2.

SECTION 1. BASIC CONCEPTS

A variety of tools are used to measure price changes taking place in an economy. These include consumer price indices (CPIs), producer price indices (PPIs), price indices relating to specific goods and/or services, and GDP deflators.

CPIs are designed to measure changes over time in average retail prices of a fixed basket of goods and services taken as representing the consumption habits of households.

PPIs provide measures of average movements of prices received by the producers of commodities. In principle, PPIs exclude transport costs and consumption taxes. Producer price indices are not a measure of average price levels, or of the costs of production. Moreover, PPIs do not include commercial mark-ups. Though the scope of PPIs varies, they are generally calculated on the basis of the total turnover of a definable industry such as manufacturing, agriculture, or mining.

In broad terms, construction price indices provide measures of changes in the prices of either the inputs to, or outputs of, construction activity. However, terminology used in the context of price indices for construction activity varies between countries. There is also considerable variation in the inclusion/exclusion of items such as transport costs, consumption taxes, fittings, etc.

A.   RELATIONSHIP OF PRODUCER PRICE INDICES TO CONSTRUCTION PRICE INDICES

Terminology Used in this Publication

For the purposes of this publication it is necessary to have a clear understanding of terminology used in the context of construction price indices. A Glossary is provided in this publication, however a number of key terms are also described below. These relate to the concept of the construction contractor, the client, purchaser, and final owner.

It should be emphasised that depending on the institutional framework operating within the construction branch of an individual country, or even for different construction projects within a country, these three concepts may relate to either separate entities, or the one organisation/individual. For example, a construction contractor building houses may also be the entity that took the initiative for the construction work. Similarly, the client may also be the final owner.

Construction contractor	A firm which undertakes works as part of a construction project by virtue of a contract with a client.
Client ("Maitre d'ouvrage")	Is the natural or legal person for whom a structure is constructed, or alternatively the person or organisation that took the initiative of the construction.
Purchaser, final owner	Is the person or organisation that pays the final seller's price. In some instances, this person or organisation may be the same as the client (refer above).

11

Elements of Construction Industry Prices

From the supply side, the price of the output of construction activity is a function of the following factors:

- *Direct inputs*: These include materials, labour, energy, etc. Direct inputs generally vary in proportion to output.

- *Indirect inputs and overheads*: These include depreciation, administrative expenses, etc. These are generally fixed and do not vary directly with the volume of output.

- *Productivity*: Refers to the efficiency with which inputs are converted into outputs (e.g. through new technical solutions, increased labour productivity, or more effective organisation of work).

- *Profit*: Is a residual determined by the sales price, and combinations of the three preceding items. Profit varies widely and may be negative.

The output price for a construction project may change for any one or more of the following reasons:

- widening or narrowing of profit margins due to changes in market conditions (i.e. irrespective of changes in costs);

- increases or decreases in the prices of direct inputs; and

- changes in productivity resulting in changes in the quantity of direct inputs per unit of output.

On the demand side, the price actually paid by the purchaser or final owner of the output of the construction activity includes a number of additional cost elements *paid by the purchaser*. These include the price of the land, costs of obtaining planning permission, taxes and connection fees, insurance, professional fees (legal, architects, engineers), real estate agent fees, land registry charges, etc.

The requested price index cost elements for deflating components of the national accounts are described in Section 1E below.

Construction Price Indices

Most of the information used in the compilation of construction price indices are derived from the *supply side* of the industry (i.e. from construction firms, sub-contractors, materials supply firms, etc.).

However, a unique feature of construction activity that impacts on the compilation of construction price indices is that in most situations the completed building or construction is not produced and sold by one construction contractor alone[1]. Normally, the client (or architect charged by the client with the responsibility of supervising the construction) concludes contracts with a number of firms. Most of these are predominantly part of the construction branch, however they may also belong to other branches of the economy (e.g. steel construction, manufacture of fixtures, engineering, etc.).

The client (or supervising architect) invites construction contractors (who in turn may invite sub-contractors) to undertake work at a building or construction site. The work to be done is referred to as "work category". If the offer is accepted the work is performed and supplied to the client/architect as a "product". The work categories correspond to the "goods" or "products" observed in other price statistics.

From the perspective of the production performed by a construction contractor, the prices in question may be either the prices of the various inputs to the construction process *paid* by the construction contractor, or the prices *received* by the construction contractor from the client for the output of the construction contractor. The latter are producer prices and come close to the concept of a PPI (i.e. in the context of the construction industry the prices received by the producers of work categories). The construction contractor's sales prices of individual work categories from the construction sector are in most cases also the purchase prices of the client.

---

[1] German Federal Statistical Office, Wiesbaden, Studies on Statistics, No. 10 - Comments on the Revision of Statistics on Construction Prices, November 1959.

An example of an input index is the index of building costs compiled in Finland which monitors changes in the prices of 95 cost items using price information obtained from construction enterprises and price lists. On the other hand, the Austrian residential and non-residential building output price index records changes in the price of residential buildings by monitoring changes in 82 representative construction operations involved in their construction.

There are a number of difficulties in compiling construction price indices using practices followed in the compilation of PPIs. These include:

- The product "building" or " construction" or its components are not produced and sold by the construction industry or its various branches alone.

- Sub-contractors selling their output to establishments and enterprises of the construction industry.

- The construction branch does not only produce new buildings or construction work. It is also involved in maintenance and repair work, conversions, extensions, demolition, etc. In addition, the turnover of the construction branch contains turnover from other branches (e.g. transport, equipment hire, etc.). These types of activities are less readily observed.

As a result of these factors it is difficult to combine individual series of price relatives for construction work at new buildings in the construction industry or its individual branches, as sufficient weighting information is seldom available. This is particularly the case for classifying turnover on new construction, repairs and maintenance, etc.

However, unlike PPIs, construction price indices are not based on the total turnover of an institutionally definable sector, but on certain product categories. It is therefore difficult to produce a PPI for the construction industry. Most of the indices produced by OECD and European Union Member countries are indices of a number of branches participating in the erection of buildings, or other construction activity.

As mentioned above construction price indices may also be compiled from information on the *demand* side of the industry. This could entail collecting information on the price actually paid by the purchaser or final owner of the output of the construction activity, as in the case of the Canadian new residential housing price index. Alternatively, it could involve gathering information on a number of additional cost elements that need to be included in order to arrive at the actual price paid by the purchaser or final owner. As mentioned above, these include the price of the land, costs of obtaining planning permission, taxes and connection fees, insurance, professional fees, real estate agent fees, land registry charges, etc.

In summary, construction price indices may be described as indices compiled from:

- prices paid by the contractor for inputs to the construction process; or

- the price received for the completed output of construction activity paid by the client; or

- the selling price including *all* of the demand side cost elements paid by the purchaser or final owner.

B.   MAIN TYPES OF CONSTRUCTION PRICE INDICES

The methods used to compile construction price indices vary significantly between OECD and European Union Member countries. Individual Member countries also use a variety of methods, data sources, etc. for the different construction price indices they produce.

Three main types of construction price indices are compiled in OECD and European Union Member countries: input price indices, output price indices, and seller's price indices.

Input Price Indices

Input price indices measure changes in the price of inputs to the construction process by monitoring separately the cost of each factor. This generally entails the compilation of a weighted index of the costs of wages and materials.

Initially, representative object (e.g. a dwelling of a specific type, size, style, etc.) is taken and the quantity of labour hours and materials needed for its construction calculated. These quantities are periodically multiplied by the corresponding prices and the outcome totalled.

Input price indices should not be used to provide information on price movements for finished construction work as they generally do not reflect the whole range of influences that impact on market prices[2]. These include changes in productivity, profit, and trade margins of the construction contractor, and changes in actual market conditions.

Input price indices only provide a reflection of changes in the prices of construction inputs. The indices produced are production cost rather than production price indices.

As a result, the real trend of building costs may differ considerably from the trend compiled solely on the basis of wages and material costs. An input

cost index is likely to overstate the price rise of completed construction work as it ignores gains in productivity reflected in price reductions.

Output Price Indices

Output price indices measure changes in the prices of what is produced by entities engaged in construction activity.

Output price indices cover most of the items normally built into the price paid by purchasers or clients to entities involved in producing the completed output of the construction activity. These generally include materials, labour, equipment hire, land preparation costs, bathroom/kitchen fittings, overheads, profits, and trade margins.

Several different techniques are used to include all these components. One method involves the inclusion in the index of all (or as many as possible of) the individual factors involved in the construction of a dwelling, non-residential building, etc. These include overheads, profits, trade margins, and any other costs paid by the client or purchaser to the builder. An alternative method entails basing the index on the prices of actual finished constructions. Both methods are described in detail below in the typology of methods used to compile construction price indices.

Seller's Price Indices

Seller's price indices measure changes in the prices of construction output paid by the purchaser or final owner of the output of construction activity.

The term "seller's price" is used to distinguish it from the "purchasers' price" as defined in the System of National Accounts (SNA). The latter (which is discussed in more detail in Section 1E below) excludes the land component in the ownership transfer.

Seller's price indices described in this publication cover the total sales price of completed construction, including not only the cost of labour and materials, but also land, direct and indirect

---

[2] University of Geneva, Laboratory of Applied Economics, Geneva - *Indices of Construction Prices, A Methodological Inventory,* Lynn Mackenzie, April 1994.

selling expenses, and seller's profits. House price indices compiled in the United States and Canada, and the dwelling price index compiled in Spain, are conceptually broader in item coverage than almost all input and output indices compiled in other OECD and European Union Member countries.

The resultant indices compiled in these countries for houses include most factors which influence movements in home prices. These include both supply factors such as wage rates, material costs, and productivity, and demand factors such as demographic changes, incomes, and the availability of mortgage finance. These indices are the closest approximations in item coverage to the actual price paid for construction output.

Some of these countries also compile seller's price indices excluding the land component.

The inclusion in the index of all the cost elements paid for by the final owner of the construction (particularly the land, finance costs, selling expenses) conceptually brings a seller's construction price index close to being a consumer price index.

Relation Between the Three Types of Indices

The item imposition of the three types of construction price indices is illustrated in the following diagram.

Input Price Index   Output Price Index   Seller's Price Index

Elements Paid by Contractor	Elements Paid by Client	Elements Paid by Final Owner
Materials	Materials	Materials
Labour	Labour	Labour
Plant & Equipment	Plant & Equipment	Plant & Equipment
Transport	Transport	Transport
Energy	Energy	Energy
Other Costs	Other Costs	Other Costs

| | Contractor's Profit Margins / Productivity / Overheads | Contractor's Profit Margins / Productivity / Overheads |

		VAT
		Land
		Architect's Fees
		Other Costs
		Client's Profit Margins

In practice, there is some degree of overlap in the item composition of the three types of construction price indices described above. For example, output price indices may include professional fees (such as architects, lawyers, engineers) to the extent that they are initially paid by the construction contractor and subsequently included in the output price paid by the client. The same principle applies to other cost elements. As will be further discussed in Section 3 the development of reliable construction price indices requires a thorough understanding of all stages of the construction process from the materials supply through to the sale of the completed "product" to the final owner.

Types of Construction Indices Compiled in OECD and European Union Member Countries

There is considerable variation in the type and composition of construction price indices compiled by OECD and European Union Member countries. Just over half of the more than 60 construction price indices described in Section 3 below are input indices. All except three of the remaining indices

15

are output indices compiled using either of the methodologies referred to above. The three exceptions are seller's price indices for houses compiled in the United States and Canada, and the dwelling price index compiled in Spain.

There is a continuum in the range of items included in input and output construction price indices. For input indices some countries such as Belgium include only labour and material inputs. Other countries, such as Japan also include some installation costs (e.g. water/gas/electricity supply, bathroom and kitchen fittings, etc.). At the other extreme countries such as Finland include a wide range of additional cost items such as transport of materials to the site, equipment hire, site preparation, conveyancing fees, outside fittings, etc.

There is a similar range of item inclusion/exclusion in output price indices reported by OECD and European Union Member countries, though almost all include estimates for trade margins, overheads, and profits. The main differences between the countries are in the inclusion/exclusion of professional fees and conveyancing fees.

The types of construction price indices compiled by OECD and European Union Member countries, together with the compilation methodology, and frequency of compilation are provided in the following table.

Construction Price Indices:
Types of Indices Calculated, Methods Used, and Frequency of Compilation

Country	Index Title	Type of Index	Methods Used[*]	Frequency of Compilation
Australia	Civil Engineering	Input	Standard factors	Quarterly
	Construction and renovation of privately built houses	Output	Matched models	Quarterly
	Construction of other dwellings and other buildings	Proxy output	Component cost	Monthly
Austria	Housing and estate building costs index	Input	Standard factors	Monthly
	Cost index for road construction	Input	Standard factors	Monthly
	Cost index for bridge construction	Input	Standard factors	Monthly
	Residential buildings price indices	Output	Component cost	Quarterly
	Other building price indices	Output	Component cost	Quarterly
	Output price index for road construction	Output	Component cost	Quarterly
	Output price index for bridge construction	Output	Component cost	Quarterly
	Other civil engineering work	Output	Component cost	Quarterly
Belgium	Composite construction price index	Input	Standard factors	Annually
Canada	Residential/Non-residential building input costs	Input	Standard factors	Monthly
	Electric utility construction price index	Input	Standard factors	Bi-annually
	Telecommunications plant	Input	Standard factors	Annually
	Construction union wage rates	Input	Standard factors	Monthly
	Apartment building construction	Output	Component cost	Quarterly
	Non-residential building construction price index	Output	Component cost	Quarterly
	New housing price index	Seller's	Matched models	Monthly
Denmark	Regulating price index for residential building construction	Input	Standard factors	Quarterly
	Regulating price indices for civil engineering works	Input	Standard factors	Quarterly

*   A description of these methods is provided in Section 1C below

Country	Index	Type	Method	Frequency
Finland	Index of building costs	Input	Standard factors	Monthly
	Building renovation costs index	Input	Standard factors	Monthly
France	Building construction sector indices (BT indices)	Input	Standard factors	Monthly
	Price indices for civil engineering sector (TP indices)	Input	Standard factors	Monthly
	Construction price indices for residential buildings (ICC)	Output	Schedule of prices	Quarterly
Germany	Conventional construction price indices	Output	Component cost	Quarterly
	Standard house price indices	Output	PPI	Bi-annually
Greece	Input materials for the construction of new residential buildings	Input	Standard factors	Quarterly
	Work categories for the construction of new buildings	Output	Component cost	Quarterly
Iceland	Index for privately built apartments	Input	Standard factors	Monthly
Ireland	Housebuilding cost index	Input	Standard factors	Monthly
	Wholesale prices index of materials	Input	Standard factors	Monthly
	Capital goods price index	Input	Standard factors	Monthly
Italy	Costs index for a residential building	Input	Standard factors	Monthly
	Cost index for a building for industrial use	Input	Standard factors	Quarterly
	Cost index for stretches of road	Input	Standard factors	Quarterly
Japan	Construction price index	Input	Standard factors	Monthly
Luxembourg	Price index for the construction of residential and semi residential buildings	Output	Component cost	Bi-annually
Mexico	Price index for social housing	Input	Standard factors	Monthly
Netherlands	Price indices for social rented housing	Output	Component cost	Monthly
	Hedonic price index for the low rent residential building sector	Output	Hedonic	Monthly
New Zealand	Input index for the construction sector	Input	Standard factors (largely)	Quarterly
	Output index for the construction sector	Output	Component cost (largely)	Quarterly
	Capital goods price index for the construction sector	Output	Component cost (largely)	Quarterly
Norway	Cost indices for residential buildings	Input	Standard factors	Monthly
	Construction cost indices for civil engineering works	Input	Standard factors	Quarterly
	Construction price index for detached houses	Output	Hedonic	Quarterly
Portugal	Construction Cost Indices	Input	Standard factors	Monthly
Spain	Construction cost index	Input	Standard factors	Quarterly
	Average prices of dwellings per square meters	Seller's	Building volume or area	Quarterly
Sweden	Factor price index for residential buildings	Input	Standard factors	Monthly
	Factor price indices for repair and maintenance of multi-dwelling, and agricultural buildings	Input	Standard factors	Monthly
	Output price indices for houses and apartments	Output	Hedonic	Monthly
Turkey	Building construction cost index	Input	Standard factors	Quarterly

Country	Index Title	Type of Index	Methods Used	Frequency of Compilation
United Kingdom	Construction materials cost index	Input	Standard factor	Monthly
	Construction industry price index of average earnings	Input	Standard factors	Monthly
	Public sector housebuilding price index	Output	Component cost	Quarterly
	Public sector non-housing price index	Output	Schedule of prices	Quarterly
	Road construction tender price index	Output	Schedule of prices	Quarterly
	Commercial and industrial building tender price index	Output	Schedule of prices	Monthly
	Output price indices	Output	Derived from above	Quarterly
United States	Price index for highway construction	Output	Component cost	Quarterly
	Cost index for large projects	Output	Component cost	Quarterly
	Price index for new one family houses	Seller's	Hedonic	Monthly

C. TYPOLOGY OF METHODS USED BY OECD AND EUROPEAN UNION MEMBER COUNTRIES FOR COMPILING CONSTRUCTION PRICE INDICES

Several different methods are used by OECD and European Union Member countries to compile construction price indices. Each method aims at minimising the problems of comparability between different constructions and comparisons over time.

Most commonly, these entail the selection of one or more standard (or model) types of construction on the assumption they are representative of all construction projects for that type of construction activity (house, apartment, factory office building, etc.). The model constructions may actually exist, or be fictitious. Each model construction is defined in great detail in order to be able to obtain the prices (either actual or notional) of all or some of the work entailed in their construction. Prices are then obtained from a number of sources. These include surveying construction companies, professional associations, administrative sources, etc.

The use of model types of construction projects is more difficult for civil engineering, where diversity, between even the same category of projects, makes the selection of "standard" constructions more difficult[3]. Methods used for this type of construction activity include analysis of the composition of expenditure by civil engineering contractors on major construction projects, expenditures being classified according to the purpose of the construction project, e.g. roads, bridges, dams, etc.

Seven construction price index compilation methods used either currently, or in the recent past, by Member countries are described below. In order to demonstrate the main principles more effectively these descriptions only contain the main elements of each methodology. In practice, the more than 60 construction price indices described in Section 3 involve numerous variants and combinations of the seven compilation methodologies described. The compilation methods (primarily) used for each of

the construction price indices calculated in Member countries are listed in the table in Section 1B above.

Prior Breakdown Methods[4]

The starting point for prior breakdown methods is a list of carefully specified factors or components, from which the total input or output costs of a building or construction project are built up.

Standard Factors: This method is mainly used for the compilation of input price indices. For any given year a representative construction (or small number of projects) is selected and the quantities of each factor used to build it (e.g. materials, labour, transport, machinery, etc.) evaluated.

Changes in the costs of construction are determined by monitoring the cost of each factor. The representative building or construction chosen initially is used only to establish the weights.

This methodology, which yields a construction cost index rather than a construction price index, is used by several OECD and European Union Member countries. As mentioned earlier there is considerable variation in the range of items included.

Component cost method: This approach is used for the compilation of output price indices. It regards construction output as bundles of standardised homogeneous components. These components correspond to the supply of standard operations (cf. Glossary). Examples would be: the supply and laying of so many square metres of roofing tiles; installation of a hot water tank of a given capacity; construction of so many square metres of brick wall etc.

Price indices are compiled using the prices of these homogenous components. A representative

---

[3] University of Geneva, Laboratory of Applied Economics, Geneva - *Indices of Construction Prices, A Methodological Inventory,* Lynn Mackenzie, April 1994.

[4] Institut National de la Statistique et des Etudes Economiques (INSEE), Paris, *Bloc-Notes 4/1990 - France's Cost of Construction Index,* Vincent le Calonnec, 1990.

construction (or number of projects) is also chosen. However, the actual work entailed in its completion is broken down into precisely defined standard services or components.

A number of representative construction firms that have recently performed any of these services are surveyed to determine the price they have actually agreed or invoiced for these services. A price index is then created for each standard component.

These indices are then aggregated for the buildings initially defined as the benchmarks. The actual buildings are used only to define a selection of services and the corresponding weights.

A variant of this approach involves the re-specification of a number of the representative projects on a cyclical basis.

The difference between an index based on input factors and one based on standard components is essentially one of degree, since components are only factors at a more advanced stage of production. However, the standard component cost index also incorporates productivity gains and changes in profit margins, as it reflects not only the cost of the factors, but also the price of the finished product paid by the customers of the construction firm. It will therefore include more of the price elements listed above that determine the prices of finished construction work.

Another advantage of this method is that the prices obtained are for components which remain comparable over time. Fluctuations due to differential quality or execution are eliminated. However, while components are more homogeneous than completed buildings it is unlikely that they will be completely identical for different completed buildings.

If there is a permanent change in the way a component is performed its definition is changed, and the new price series is spliced to the old one by means of chaining taking account of changes in quality.

Selecting truly representative standard components, and determining weighting coefficients that accurately reflect construction techniques and the way buildings, etc. are usually constructed during the base year is the hardest and most important part of compiling the index. However, every standard component does not have to be priced separately. For example, if the price change characteristics of brick laying and paving are similar then prices of only one of (similar) standard components need to be incorporated in the construction price index.

An advantage of both the standard factor and standard component cost methods is that they can produce different indices merely by changing the weighting of the indices for each component. For example, indices could be compiled by type of work, by trade, or as in the example of the conventional construction price indices compiled in Germany, by type of building.

Subsequent Breakdown Methods

Subsequent breakdown methods involve the use of samples of either actually completed, or fictitious construction projects. They entail the collection of prices effectively charged (or what would be charged) by the builder and incorporate changes in productivity and profit margins. These methods start from the "completed" building or project which are then broken down into component parts.

These methods are used primarily for the compilation of output price indices. The hedonic and matched model methods outlined below are also used by Member countries to compile seller's price indices.

Quoted prices: In this method the problem of comparability of components between construction projects is overcome by having respondents quote prices for a standard construction output product (house, apartment, bridge, school, etc.) whose specifications are kept constant from one period to the next.

For example, the detailed specifications for a house (of specific type, style, size, etc.) are distributed to a sample of building firms. Bids or quotes are then collected for the entire building as specified, as well as the electrical work in the specifications, the brick work, etc. Respondents are asked to bid as though they were tendering for real work, taking account of prevailing market conditions and costs. The bids for each component are averaged and weighted up to an overall price, and a price index is computed.

The standard construction (house, apartment, bridge, school, etc.) is updated periodically to reflect changes in materials, styles, etc. to ensure that it is typical of those being constructed at the time.

A major problem with this method is that it is difficult for firms to take the process seriously. They are not bidding for real work and there is no bargaining involved.

Schedule of prices: This method entails the selection of a representative sample of construction projects either taking place, or completed, in a given geographic area, over a specified period of time. The cost of each technical component (derived from blueprints, work specifications, etc.) of a given construction in the sample is priced as at the base reference date. This involves the use of a schedule of prices containing the price of each component of the construction at the base period date. Examples of this method are the construction price indices for residential buildings compiled in France, and several output price indices compiled in the United Kingdom.

By aggregating the prices for all the components a theoretical average price of the entire construction is obtained as though it had been undertaken at the base reference date. The general weighting is obtained from statistics on current construction. A price index is then obtained by calculating the ratio of the current actual price of the sampled construction to the recalculated price at the base reference period (derived from the sum of its components compiled from the schedule of prices).

The role of the schedule of prices is to define a price structure, not the average level of each component. The composition of the schedule of prices may not necessarily reflect the average prices for the base period. Obtaining such an average would require a very large sample. However, the relative structure of the prices on the schedule reflects market conditions at the time period in question.

Matched models: Involves the specification of a sample of representative construction projects (or models), the matching of these "model" projects against actual projects carried out by contractors in a specified period, the collection of prices for the matched projects for each period, and the weighting together of price movements for each project. Constant quality is maintained by calculating price movements on a matched sample basis (i.e. the price movements between adjacent periods are based on the same "model" projects each period).

This methodology is used for the calculation of price indices for standard project home construction, as in the case of the price indices for the construction and renovation of privately built houses compiled in Australia. The composition of the list of construction projects or "models" to be matched against actual construction projects is subject to continuous review, and is determined by the continued availability of price information relating to a particular model specification. If the specification of an individual model changes significantly, or if a price is unable to be obtained, then that model is excluded from the calculation of price movement.

Price information for the actual finished construction is obtained for each period from a sample of builders/construction firms, real estate organisations, government agencies, etc. They relate to actual sales transacted during the period.

Building volume or area[5]: For this index the cubic metre is used as a common denominator to compare the costs of a recent construction to costs in a base period. An index of the value per cubic metre is calculated and adjusted for differences in volume, quality, period, and region. These adjustments enable a price index to be prepared. However, the use of this method requires the construction activity included to be homogenous. The index is valid only for each reference building, etc. as it was originally built.

This method is no longer used by any Member country in its pure form, however building volume is used in some countries (by the Netherlands for

---

[5] Central Bureau of Statistics Netherlands, Voorburg - *A Hedonic Approach to Output Indices for Construction,* George van Leeuwen, February 1995.

University of Geneva, Laboratory of Applied Economics, Geneva - *Indices of Construction Prices, A Methodological Inventory,* Lynn Mackenzie, April 1994.

example) as one of the building characteristics in the regression analysis used in the compilation of the hedonic construction price indices described below.

A variant of this method used in the compilation of an output price index for dwellings in Spain uses the average price per square metre as one of the variables collected in determining the average prices of monitored dwellings.

Hedonic method: Regression techniques may be used to construct hedonic indices to measure purchasers' preferences for the different characteristics of construction work. This approach, which is used in the compilation of some of the price indices compiled in the Netherlands, Sweden and the United States, starts from the premise that each construction is a combination of characteristics, each of which has an implicit price. This price is set by the market and is reflected in the over-all prices for which different combinations of these characteristics are sold, and where different varieties of the same construction type, each with its own peculiar combination of characteristics, co-exist.

In addition to total price a limited number (7 to 15) of characteristics (qualitative or quantitative) are taken into account. For a house, possible characteristics include: floor area, number of floors, type of garage, method of heating, number of toilets, etc.

Using econometric techniques (regression and covariance analysis) weight of each of these characteristics in determining the price is estimated. These weights can then be used to factor out that part of the price change in the next month which is due to changes in the characteristics of the house, etc. sold. The coefficients of the regressions are calculated first by means of total construction price information and their characteristics in the current year, and on the basis of information on the same type for a base period.

Each construction during the current period is priced at what it would have cost during the reference period, once its characteristics are known. Indices are calculated from current prices and then aggregated using either Laspeyres formula if the values of the characteristics are taken from the base period, or Paasche if they are taken from the current period.

The problem with this method, which is based on just a few elements of construction, is that it is less discerning than the schedule of prices method in detecting qualitative change. If construction quality is enhanced the improvement will tend to be underestimated and thus the actual increase in prices overestimated.

Furthermore, the use of these techniques requires the statistical agency to have access to trained econometricians, as well as specialist knowledge of the construction industry.

D.   OUTLINE OF PROCESSES IN DEVELOPING A CONSTRUCTION PRICE INDEX

As with both CPIs and PPIs, the development and compilation of price indices for construction activity is a complex procedure consisting of a long and varied set of operations. The usefulness of the construction indices compiled also depends on having a clear understanding of the purposes of the indices, and the characteristics of the construction industry in the country where it is located. These characteristics include:

- the range of construction activities conducted throughout the country;

- construction techniques commonly used for each type of construction activity, together with an idea of the rate of change in techniques used;

- types of entities/organisations undertaking construction activity, and their characteristics (e.g. size, industry concentration, etc.);

- administrative arrangements for the maintenance of building/construction standards;

- administrative arrangements for government authorisation of individual construction projects.

These aspects must be determined before commencement of work on the creation of the index. Relevant characteristics of the country external to the construction industry also need to be identified. These could be economic, demographic, geographic, or administrative.

The major processes in the development and compilation of construction price indices using the "model price" methodology outlined above are:

- Selection of a small, representative group of recently constructed buildings, civil engineering projects, etc. as models. The number of models required depends on the range of construction activity to be included in the index, diversity of the specifications for each type of activity, and regional diversity .

- Specification of the hundreds of detailed tasks or component trades in the construction of these model projects. These are prepared using architectural drawings and specifications. Also involves the development of components for the general requirements (overheads and profit margins) of the main construction contractor.

- Selection of a sample of components. The selection of components within each trade area is based on both money value and the coverage of significant materials and/or products involved. A goal might be to select components which cover at least 70 per cent of the total value of the trade.

- Development of specifications for each component to include quantities involved and base-weight unit prices. Specifications must be exact to avoid the risk of varying interpretation by different respondents.

- Selection of a sub-sample of subcontractors and general contractors in the appropriate geographic areas from whom prices are collected. An important goal is to select contractors who are actively engaged in building sample components and can report price quotes based on recent experience. Some respondents might be able to supply quotes on components included in more than one model.

- Collection of periodic reports for a sample of these components from subcontractors. These should be based on current prices they charge (including overheads and profit) for the component they supply. Price collection may be done by telephone or mail, generally after an initial personal visit to gain co-operation and discuss reporting problems. The prices of electrical and mechanical equipment can be obtained from manufacturers of the equipment.

- Calculation of a price index for the construction as a weighted combination of these component prices. This is done by multiplying new price quotations by base period weights, and comparing the result to base period model prices.

- Development and implementation of an on-going process of index review to revise the list of model projects, weights, component items, respondents, etc.

It could take as long as year to set up the models, enlist respondents, and begin to collect data.

Further information on each of these processes is provided below in Section 2 of this publication.

E.   USES OF CONSTRUCTION PRICE INDICES

Construction price indices are primarily used for analysis of price movements and price formation in the construction industry, for price escalation clauses in construction contracts, and for deflation of components of the national accounts.

More specifically, the primary uses are[6]:

---

[6] German Federal Statistical Office, Wiesbaden, *Detailed indices for Construction Prices and Construction Work,* Series 4, May 1994.

- Measuring the changes of prices of construction materials for construction work.

  In developing a program of projects, preparing estimates, comparing estimates with bids, and scheduling projects within funding limits it is necessary to have some way of judging price movements. The aim is to express physical volumes of work needed for future construction work in value terms.

- Studying the impacts of changing prices over the total construction cost and selling prices of the construction work.

- Measuring the expenditure of consumed materials at constant prices.

- Estimating the short-term evolution of prices.

- To determine replacement values for insurance purposes.

  The use of construction price indices (where quality and other changes in the price determining characteristics of the construction operations observed have been eliminated) can have considerable impact if they are used to determine replacement values. If construction work of the original quality is no longer supplied because of substantial changes in materials, techniques, etc. the replacement values obtained from the use of construction price indices may be considerably less than the amount actually required to be spent on the replacement.

- Realising price-index readjustments of construction contracts.

- Planning the production of materials and checking the efficiency of entrepreneurial units.

- Deflating components of the national accounts. In addition to the compilation of national accounts at current prices there is a necessity in having constant price measures that separate the effects of price and volume increases (or decreases). This necessity is particularly strong in countries experiencing high inflation.

Use of Construction Price Indices for Deflating Components of National Accounts

National accounts constant value estimates are usually made by deflating estimates in current values by appropriate price indices at as fine a level of detail as possible and adding up the results. The aim of such calculations is to enable the analysis of period-to-period changes, by separating GDP and its sub-aggregates into distinct price and volume components.

One of the main problems in the compilation of price indices for national accounts deflation purposes is that of ensuring that an appropriate price index is used for the national account item being deflated. In the context of construction price indices the issue is primarily one of matching the national account item being deflated with the item coverage of the price indices used. The former primarily involves the deflation of construction industry output and/or gross fixed capital formation (GFCF). The deflation of these components of the national accounts by OECD and European Union Member countries often entails the use of different construction price indices.

The System of National Accounts (SNA) makes the distinction between two types of prices for valuing output: basic prices; and producer's prices.

- The *basic price* is the amount receivable by the producer from the purchaser for a unit of good or service produced as output minus any tax payable, and plus any subsidy receivable, on that unit as a consequence of its production or sale.

- The *producer's price* is the amount receivable by the producer from the purchaser for a unit of a good or service produced as output minus any VAT, or similar deductible tax, invoiced to the purchaser.

Both prices exclude transport charges invoiced separately by the producer.

The preferred basis of valuation for deflating construction industry output is at basic prices, though producer's prices may be used when valuation at basic prices is not feasible. The European System of National and Regional

24

Accounts in the European Community (ESA) specifies that only basic prices may be used.

Care should be taken to ensure consistency between the valuation of industry output and the valuation of the price index used for deflation.

For all transactions on the uses of goods and services such as final consumption, intermediate consumption, and capital formation) both the SNA and the ESA specify purchaser's prices as the preferred basis of valuation.

The *purchaser's price* is the amount paid by the purchaser, excluding any deductible VAT or similar deductible tax, in order to take delivery of a unit of a good or service at the time and place required by the purchaser. This price includes transport charges paid separately by the purchaser to take delivery.

Therefore, on the expenditure side a purchaser's price index is required for the deflation of items of construction falling within GFCF. For new fixed assets these include not only all transport and installation changes but also the costs incurred in the transfer of ownership, in the form of fees paid to surveyors, engineers, architects, lawyers, estate agents etc., and any taxes payable on the transfer.

Output construction price indices compiled by Member countries include a number of cost elements to enable the index to approximate basic, producer's, or purchaser's prices as defined in the SNA. The essential differences between the three price valuations being the inclusion or exclusion of taxes, subsidies, and transport charges.

Due to the lack of suitable available output price indices some countries use input price indices for deflation purposes. Some use these indices making allowance for productivity change, variations in profits, and incorporation of overheads.

Seller's price indices which include cost items outside the scope of the production account for construction, and GFCF (in particular the cost of the land) may be less suitable for national account deflation purposes.

SECTION 2. CONSTRUCTION PRICE INDEX COMPILATION ISSUES

A. IMPORTANT CONSIDERATIONS IN THE COMPILATION OF CONSTRUCTION PRICE INDICES

Most of the procedures involved in the development and calculation of construction price indices (outlined in Section 1D above) are similar to those used in the compilation of CPIs and PPIs. However, listed below are a number of problem areas that are either unique to construction activity, or where particular attention is required when construction price indices are developed. These issues are described in more detail in Section 2D.

Diversity of Construction Activity

To portray price changes by means of a price index it is important for the data to relate to types of work that remain constant. The main problem in the compilation of price indices for construction arises from the fact that the products/outputs of construction activity (houses, apartments, factories, schools, bridges, dams, etc.) are seldom exactly comparable with one another. Differences arise due to variations in the plans/specifications, production location (building site), etc. for each product. Civil engineering and non-residential building outputs are particularly heterogeneous.

The range of compilation methods used to minimise the impact of this diversity are outlined in Sections 1B and 1C above. These include pricing components rather than the entire construction project and the selection of individual types of work (or model) that regularly occur.

Another factor to consider is the type of construction activity to include in the scope of the index. Both the components, and the relative use of these components (weights) vary significantly between each type of construction activity. Each construction price index relates to predetermined types of construction activity and care is required to avoid the use of indices for unrelated types of construction work.

Changes Over Time

Given that both the inputs to, and outputs of construction activity constantly change, another problem in compiling construction price indices is that of ensuring comparability over time. Factors that influence such change include size, finish, style, equipment used, fashions, etc. This problem does not exist to the same extent for consumer items where a price index can be compiled immediately for the entire period over which such products, their quality unchanged, are sold.

To ensure that the values reported for a particular price series will show only "pure" price changes all the factors contributing to a price level (the so-called price determining characteristics) must be kept constant as long as possible.

One method commonly used by OECD and European Union Member countries to compare two or more construction projects (which are always different), involves breaking the projects down into elementary components that are more comparable over time.

Selection of Appropriate Prices

The selection of the appropriate price is also an important consideration in the development of a construction price index. The following types of price data are generally available for construction activity[7]:

- tender prices
- prices at the time of award of contract
- invoice prices

Obtaining the "right" transaction price as opposed to list prices, the lowest price, etc. is critical. List prices for example need to be adjusted for:

---

[7] Austrian Central Statistical Office, Vienna, Statistische Nachrichten - *Index of Building Prices.*

26

- cash discounts;
- competitive discounts;
- seasonal discounts;
- trade discounts (i.e. a discount made to a certain class of buyer);
- quantity discounts.

A difficulty with one type of model pricing is that contractors may be asked to provide hypothetical prices, what they would charge, rather than actual transaction prices. It is also difficult to ensure that the prices compiled reflect current market conditions and include a realistic allowance for overheads and profit.

Finally, as with other types of price indices, it is also difficult to separate changes in price from changes in quality. The latter may occur when a builder or subcontractor alters the way that component is supplied, for example through the use of a new material or new equipment.

A prerequisite for dealing with this issue is to have staff with detailed knowledge of the construction industry to ensure that price information provided by material suppliers, construction contractors, etc. can be evaluated for reasonableness, and who can ask probing questions where necessary. Price collection staff must also be particularly alert to changes in the quality of components.

Range of Items for Inclusion

As mentioned in Section 1B above there is considerable variation in the type and number of items included, even for the same types of indices, compiled by OECD and European Union Member countries.

The construction of a building or civil engineering project often involves thousands of complex operations and components. In developing a construction price index a decision is required on the number and types of items to include to ensure that the resulting index will accurately reflect price changes. The choice of items to be included in a particular index is strongly influenced by the type of index being compiled (input, output, seller's), and its purpose. For example, if the primary purpose of the index is to deflate components of the national accounts, the item coverage of the index

should match the scope/content of the national account component being deflated.

Another consideration in compiling each type of construction price index is the need to distinguish between the items paid by the producer (the contractor) and those paid by the purchaser or final owner.

Items considered for inclusion or exclusion in any specific index are profits, overheads, margins, the price of land, site preparation, architects and supervisors fees, transport, legal fees, certain types of installations (central heating, elevators, cable television systems, garages, etc.). The EUROSTAT publication *Industrial Short Term Indicators - Methodology* outlines recommendations, rules and regulations concerning the composition of short term indicators (including construction price indices) for European Union Member countries.

To compile indices comparable between European Union member countries EUROSTAT recommends the inclusion/exclusion of the following elements for the three types of construction price indices described in Section 1 of this publication.

- *Input:* Should include at least the prices of raw materials and wages paid by the construction contractor, though not changes in the contractor's productivity and profits, or the price of land, architects fees, etc. Input indices can also include other input factors such as equipment, transport or energy.

- *Output:* Should include prices paid by the contractor for all factors contributing to the construction activity paid by the client. These should include those listed previously for inclusion in input indices, plus changes in productivity, profits. Output indices should not include elements not normally paid by the client. These could include the price of land, architects fees, etc.

- *Sellers:* Should include all the elements included in both input and output price indices plus the price of land, and other elements included in the total sales price of the completed construction paid by the purchaser or final owner.

Ensuring Geographic Representativeness of the Index

Regional differences can have a major impact on costs, prices, size, style (single dwelling versus multiple dwelling constructions, low versus high density dwellings, etc.), construction materials used, methods used, etc. It is particularly important to identify any rural/urban differences. If an index is to be applied nationally there is a need to ensure that regional differences are represented in the price collection process, and that the index is compiled with the appropriate weights reflecting these differences.

Types of Construction Firms to Include

Construction activity may be conducted by specialised businesses predominantly engaged in construction, either as prime contractors responsible for the entire project, or sub-contractors involved in specific (and specialised) trades. Construction activity may also be carried out by businesses classified to other industries, or by government. At the other extreme, construction activity (particularly house construction) may be undertaken by individuals for their own use (i.e. owner-builders).

The materials, construction techniques used, and even the type of construction activity undertaken, may vary according to the type of entity involved in the construction activity.

In transition economies there is a particular need to ensure that data collection is extended to the newly emerging private organisations (and new configurations of old enterprises), as well as state-owned enterprise. In other words, price data must be obtained from organisations representative of the whole range of construction activity. For example, selection of only the largest enterprises currently operating might result in the emerging private sector (which may only comprise smaller entities) being under-represented, or omitted altogether.

Related to the issue of the type of construction firms, etc. to include in the collection of price information is inclusion or exclusion of foreign contractors, or domestic contractors working abroad. Consideration needs to be given as to whether or not the price information obtained reflects the price change characteristics of the country in which the index is being compiled.

B.   PARTICULAR PROBLEMS/ISSUES FOR TRANSITION COUNTRIES

Many transition countries are currently developing their own construction price indices, or plan to develop these indices in the near future. In addition to the problems faced by market economies outlined above, transition countries need to take a number of particular issues and concerns unique to their situation into consideration. These include:

- The inclusion of construction activities in the price indices that are experiencing particularly dramatic growth during the transition period. These include the construction of hotels, shops, and private residential buildings. Whilst small in numbers these types of construction could be significant in terms of the gross output of the construction industry. At the same, work on major new state projects has almost been completely suspended in many transition countries.

- Movement away from the dominance of the construction industry by large state enterprises

by the entry of a larger number of smaller and perhaps more specialised construction enterprises, e.g. firms specialising in the installation of fittings in newly restituted shops, building of private houses, etc. Related to this issue is the need for transition countries to develop techniques/procedures, questionnaires, etc. to obtain the required price information from construction enterprises (of all sizes) in the emerging private sector.

- The inclusion of construction activity carried out by unauthorised persons.

- The inclusion of barter arrangements between construction enterprises.

C.   SOURCES OF INFORMATION USED TO COMPILE CONSTRUCTION PRICE INDICES

From the perspective of the organisation responsible for compiling a construction price index the selection of the most appropriate sources of information used depends on a number of considerations. These include the use(s) to which the index will be put and the type of index required (input, output), data availability, and resources (both financial and skill) available in the organisation. The institutional background in which a construction price index will be developed, will to a large extent determine the feasibility and cost of the index, and influence the methodology used in its compilation.

The data required to compile an index may be in the form of price information obtained from construction enterprises or materials suppliers. Alternatively, components of the price index may be obtained from administrative agencies charged by law with the responsibility for compiling basic costs indices, or by professional associations for use as benchmarks for contracts in the profession. Information may also be obtained from the client who may be traced through building permits.

The following table summarises possible sources of information for compiling construction price indices.

Types of Information Required for Price Index	Possible Data Sources
Input prices - materials	• Surveys of construction, building material supply, or building material manufacturing enterprises.
	• Associations of quantity surveyors
	• Trade associations
	• Chambers of commerce
	• Other national statistical office collections (e.g. for producer price indices
	• Government agencies charged with responsibility of monitoring capital construction works (particularly roads, dams, bridges, etc.)
Input prices - labour	• Trade unions
	• Trade associations
	• Collective bargaining agreements registered with government
	• Government agencies charged with responsibility for regulating wages.
	• Enterprise surveys of employers
	• Household surveys of employees
Transport costs	• Transport associations
	• Surveys of transport enterprises
	• Relevant government agencies
Weight information	• Construction branch structural enterprise surveys
	• Associations of quantity surveyors
	• Architectural enterprises/associations

The actual sources of information used by OECD and European Union Member countries in the compilation of specific construction price indices are listed in Country Summary Table 1.

D. MAJOR ELEMENTS OF CONSTRUCTION PRICE INDICES

The major elements of construction price indices are outlined below. These elements are interrelated in the sense that a series of trade-offs and adjustments are made between them by the organisation developing the index. These trade-offs are largely determined by the proposed use of the index, data availability, and resources available for developing and compiling the index. For example, in the case of a price index for house construction, the requirement for an index encompassing both rural and urban areas of a country might for cost reasons be traded off in favour of including only urban house construction by a decision to include price information for a larger number work categories, materials, etc. Such a trade-off could be justified, for example in countries where an overwhelmingly large proportion of house construction takes place in urban areas.

Construction Type/Activity Coverage

The decision by OECD and European Union Member countries on the types of construction or construction activities to include in the construction price index (or indices) they compile largely depends on the use(s) of the completed index. Some countries compile special purpose indices covering a very narrow range of construction types (e.g. one family houses in the United States, social housing in Mexico, bridge construction in Austria, etc.), whilst others compile separate indices for all, or almost all, construction activities (e.g. Austria and Australia). A number of Member countries compile a weighted composite index of all construction types (e.g. Belgium and Japan). Finally, some indices include only construction types undertaken on behalf public or private sector clients (e.g. the index for privately built apartments in Iceland).

Several characteristics of activities undertaken in the construction sector result in difficulties in compiling construction price indices. These characteristics include:

- the fact that the resultant indices are mainly not based on the total turnover of an institutionally definable sector, but on product categories (or types of construction);

- the production of these types of construction works (residential buildings, non-residential buildings, roads, etc.) by several industry branches; and

- the inclusion of these activities (joinery, steel construction, etc.) in other branches of the economy.

The type of entity (construction material supplier, construction contractor) to be priced will vary according to the use(s) of the construction price index, and the type of index being compiled (input, output, seller's). If used to deflate components of the national accounts, the item content of the index should as far as possible, correspond to the value coverage of the national account item to be deflated. Alternatively, if the index is to be used to re-adjust long-term contracts, the types of construction projects included in the index should match construction activities for which contracts are to be indexed. This may not be possible in a single construction price index, and it may be necessary to compile a number of indices. Alternatively, it may be necessary to use one index that best fits all or most of the uses, or from which most of the purposes can be met.

The compilation of price indices to portray the movement of prices across all construction types involves the selection of individual projects from each type of construction. The impact of the diversity (particularly non-residential building and civil engineering projects) of construction activity on price change is reduced by selecting a number of representative projects from each construction type. Some countries select projects carried out over a number of years to eliminate any bias that might occur if a shorter period were chosen.

Matching the construction types or activities to be included in the index with proposed use(s) of the index entails use of a combination of different classifications to define the activity, industries, occupation, type of construction, etc. that are incorporated in the index. The mix of classifications used varies between each Member country, and between the different construction price indices compiled in each of these countries.

A number of countries have developed their own classifications to take account of local conditions, institutional/administrative arrangements, and work practices. In almost all instances these national classifications are compatible with standard international classifications. These include:

- General classifications of industries (NACE Rev. 1; ISIC Rev. 3): According to which enterprises are classified.

- Classification by type of constructions (residential buildings, non-residential buildings, civil engineering, etc.), for example the draft EUROSTAT Classification of Types of Constructions: Very often, different indices are calculated for each of the main types of construction.

- Classification by trade or occupation (carpenters, bricklayers, plumbers, etc.), for example the International Standard Classification of Occupations (ISCO): The wage component used in input prices is often obtained from existing indices compiled by trade associations, etc.

- Classification by construction work categories (brick works, marble tiling).

- Classifications of geographic areas.

It is recommended that countries developing construction price indices use either international classifications, or nationally developed classifications that are compatible with international classifications. Extracts from some of these international classifications showing areas relevant to construction price indices are provided in Section 5 of this publication.

Geographic Coverage

Some OECD and European Union Member countries compile national construction price indices from the (weighted) average of a set of regional indices, whilst others compile regional indices from national indices. The need to observe construction prices across capital cities, towns, villages and rural areas depends on the extent to which price changes differ in each of the regions. It also depends on the resources available to develop regional indices and to collect regional price data.

Where regional price trends do not differ substantially, it is sufficient merely to distinguish metropolitan areas, other large cities, small cities, villages, and rural areas. Some countries (e.g. Greece) compile indices only in respect of capital cities, on the assumption they are representative of the urban areas for the entire country. Where regional differences are important a good geographical dispersion is important. Ignoring the problem can lead to quite misleading results, especially where a large portion of the population lives in rural areas.

It is recommended that national price indices be compiled as averages of regional price indices and not as indices of national price averages. In other words, for each regional price observed a price relative would be computed showing the change from one period to the next. These price relatives would then be averaged over the whole country. As a result only the price changes occurring within regions would influence the national average. Examples of the aggregation of regional indices to obtain national indices include the residential building, and buildings for industrial use input indices compiled in Italy, and the residential building output price indices compiled in Austria.

Indices compiled in some countries take account of differences in the types of terrain where construction activity takes place. Examples of this are the output price indices for road, bridge, and other civil engineering construction compiled in Austria where the weights distinguish between flat, hilly, and mountainous terrain.

In some countries separate indices can be compiled only for very large geographic regions, and in some instances it is not possible to produce any regional indices. Whether this is important again depends on the extent of regional variation in price changes over time.

Items in the Index

The primary purpose for the collection of prices of categories of work, materials, etc. for construction activity is to record the changes to which these prices are subject over time. The absolute prices provided by respondents are only used for the calculation of a series of relatives.

As mentioned in Section 1B above, there are considerable differences in the types of items included in the compilation of construction price indices by OECD and European Union Member countries. There are also considerable differences in the number of items actually priced, ranging from a few dozen to several thousand.

Determining the actual items to include in the index is largely a matter of judgement. The compilation of an index involving several thousand items could lead to high degrees of accuracy. However, it could also be difficult and costly to collect the price information for each of the items.

The objective is to identify the minimum number of indicator items that collectively represent a high proportion of the total value of the construction project. These items are referred to as indicators[8]. For civil engineering projects they could include: common excavation, structural steel; structural concrete; Portland cement concrete surfaces; etc. When there are changes in the prices of the principal work item (such as bridges, excavations, road surfacing, etc.) the prices of the indicator items usually move in the same direction, and to the same extent.

Other items considered for inclusion in the index may be surrogates, in that they will normally parallel price changes in the hundreds of other items that are not included in the price index.

The decision on whether or not to include an item in an index depends on the impact that changes in the price of that item (or group of items) may have on the total price of the construction. For example, including only the factors entailed in erecting the shell of a building might be insufficient to measure price changes for the purchaser. Finishing work (such as the installation of fittings, connection of utilities) could also have considerable impact on building prices. As a result most OECD and European Union Member countries include the prices of finishing and ancillary trades in their building indices.

Weights

Several different weights may be used in the compilation of construction price indices. These could include weights for:

- Individual branches of the construction industry if a composite index including several groups or classes is compiled. These weights could be based on the respective share of the groups or classes to total industry output in a base year.

- Different types of building construction (residential (houses, apartments); non-residential buildings (factories, schools, commercial, etc.); and civil engineering construction. These weights could be based on the value of the respective share of each type of construction to total value compiled from approval authority data.

- Geographic dissaggregations (e.g. regions, states, capital cities, rural/urban areas, etc.).

- Component item weights for which price information are collected from construction material suppliers, construction contractors, etc. These may comprise work categories, construction materials, etc. depending on the nature of the index. OECD and European Union Member countries primarily base their weights for each component item either on a single (or small number of) standard construction model, or the expenditure accounts of a representative sample of construction enterprises.

The availability of these weights enables the compilation of a variety of indices, by type of

---

[8] Federal Highway Administration, Washington D.C. - *FHWA Bid Price Index - 1987 Base Year*, C.A. Leonin, 1989.

construction activity, regional indices, and indices for different work categories/material components.

Countries calculating a construction price index on the basis of weights derived from notional typical projects use records of final costs of the selected construction projects to determine the proportion of the share of the component items to the total cost of construction in the base year. These weights are then used in subsequent periodic index calculations. The number of model projects on which weights are based varies significantly for the different indices compiled by Member countries. The Canadian apartment building construction output price index uses weights based on a single apartment building that was actually built in 1981. Austria bases the weights for its road construction output index on cost studies of around 200 road construction projects.

Countries calculating construction price indices on the basis of factor inputs or component costs, survey construction enterprises to determine the relative values of material and labour inputs or carefully defined types of construction activities during the base period. Bills of quantities or accounting records may be used to identify the appropriate inputs and their respective weights. The analyses undertaken by OECD and European Union Member countries range from subjective assessments of cost distribution derived from a relatively small number of construction enterprises, to the use of data from periodic construction industry surveys.

The impact the diversity of construction activity on price trends is reduced by calculating weights from a selection of representative types of work from a range of construction projects carried out. The production of a table of weights based either on the average shares of categories of work carried out or material components represented by individual types of work/components, is therefore independent of the nature and purpose of a particular project.

The methods used by OECD and European Union Member countries to compile weights are outlined in Country Summary Table 2.

Basis of Prices

As mentioned in Section 2A above the selection of the appropriate price is an important consideration in the development of a construction price index. The aim is to use prices that provide the closest approximation to market prices actually paid by the purchaser of the construction, component item, service, etc.

In most OECD and European Union Member countries the prices collected are net of discounts, with the exception of some of the input indices compiled in Canada, Denmark, and New Zealand. The inclusion/exclusion of VAT and other taxes shows quite wide variation.

There are generally a number of different types of prices available for construction price index compilation. These include[9]:

- *Tender prices:* Determined at the time of the submission of the tender. They can be calculated accurately, but are "theoretical" prices in that not all tenders lead to the award of a contract. In that sense tender prices may not be true market prices. The organisation commissioning the tender awards the construction project to the prime contractor/sub-contractor that submitted the best offer, both in terms of price and quality.

- *Prices at the time of award of contract:* Are prices that form the basis of agreement between the owner and the contractor at the time of signing the contract. These prices may not be identical to the tender price but usually reflect the market situation at the time in question. They have the advantage of being available very quickly for index compilation.

- *Invoice prices:* Are the prices actually paid. They are therefore an exact reflection of the remuneration received for the precisely defined work performed, construction materials, etc. The main problem in using invoice prices in index compilation is that they may not be

---

[9] Austrian Central Statistical Office, Vienna, Statistische Nachrichten - *Index of Building Prices.*

available until well beyond the "current" price period.

The use of model pricing may also involve a departure from the collection of actual market prices. The contractor may be asked to provide hypothetical prices, i.e. what they *would* charge, rather than *actual* transaction prices. It is difficult in this situation to ensure that the prices compiled reflect current market conditions, and include a realistic allowance for overheads and profit.

As mentioned previously, a prerequisite for obtaining the correct price information is to have staff with detailed knowledge of the construction industry to ensure that price information provided by material suppliers, construction contractors, etc. can be evaluated for reasonableness, and who can ask probing questions where necessary. Price collection staff must also be particularly alert to changes in the quality of components, which may occur when a builder or subcontractor alters the way that component is supplied, for example through the use of new materials or new equipment.

Price Collection

The issues involved in the collection of information for construction price indices are identical to those for PPIs and CPIs. The procedures implemented in this phase of index compilation have a major impact on the accuracy of the indices produced. The major issues include:

- *Selection of respondents:* In principle, all types of organisations involved in construction activity within the scope of the construction price index being compiled should be represented in the sample of respondents. These include large and small, private and state-owned organisations. The techniques used by Member countries for selecting respondents vary from judgmental selection, to the use of random sample selection.

- *Number of respondents:* Is essentially a sampling question. The larger the number of respondents selected, the more detailed will be the indices produced. In practice, the size of the sample is a trade-off against cost, data quality and respondent load. For example, it may be more appropriate to use resources to collect price information (by personal interview) of a higher quality from a smaller sample.

- *Number of prices collected:* It is difficult to recommend a precise number of price quotations. In theory the optimal number of price quotations per enterprise may vary depending on the size and range of price changes (price variability), and on the size of the enterprise. In many countries the average number of price quotations per enterprise is between three and five. In branches where products are homogeneous and commercial transactions simple, one quotation could be sufficient to represent all the transactions of the enterprise.

- *Item specification:* To portray price changes by means of a price index it is important that the data relate to types of work that remain constant so that hidden model and quality changes will not distort results.

The recommended basis of accurate price collection is the precise specification of the factor or component cost for which price information is obtained from the construction contractor, building material supplier, etc. For a construction material component being priced this may entail the specification including the system, brand, make, model number, type, or patent, for the item being priced[10]. An example of a component cost item specification from an Austrian output price index is:

> "1 m² of covering roof area with freshly fired clay roofing tiles ...*... cm. Product ...... laid dry, suspended/nailed on prepared battens."

An alternative procedure (used in some transition economies) of providing respondents with only functional descriptions of the items/services to be priced, in effect, allows the respondent to select the actual item priced. This approach might result in the reported prices containing a mix of quality change and pure price variation.

- *Collection method:* Options for the collection of price information are personal visit,

---

[10] Austrian Central Statistical Office, Vienna, Statistische Nachrichten - *Index of Building Prices*

collection by telephone, or mail collection. The recommended approach entails personal visit to gain the co-operation of the respondent, identify the items to be priced, firming up item specifications, and to discuss possible reporting problems and issues. Price information may then be collected by mail, telephone or electronic data interchange (EDI). However, it is also essential for respondents to be visited at frequent intervals to ensure that prices are provided strictly in accordance with the specifications, and that hidden quality changes, etc. have not crept into the price information provided.

The selection of strictly specified transactions in the initial phase of respondent recruitment also requires use of the expertise of representatives of the respondent organisation. The information required from the respondent during the initial visit includes the selection of a representative set of transactions to be priced each month, quarter, etc. This is normally based on a judgmental approach using the advice of the respondent.

Finally, in order to ensure that the item being priced adheres to the specification provided, provision should be made for the respondent to report changes in the actual specifications of the item reported. It is also necessary to determine whether any changes are temporary or permanent.

Index Review

Irrespective of the method used for their derivation, the weights for the various components of construction price indices should be characteristic of the periods being compared. As time goes by indices lose their relevance as building practices and technology diverge more and more from those prevailing in the base period (the period to which the weights relate), whose weights continue to be used. As a result, weights for construction price indices need to be reviewed, and where necessary revised at least every five to ten years.

The frequency of the revisions is largely dependent on the pace of structural and technological change taking place in the construction industry in any particular country. For example, the rapid institutional, administrative, and technological

changes taking place in transition countries could justify revisions every three to five years.

More specifically, changes to the weights are required because of:

- shifts in construction methods and practices from one base year to the next;

- differential price trends between trades;

- structural differences in the make-up of samples of buildings constructed during the reference period, e.g. use of more energy efficient designs.

Another objective of index review is to ease the task of reporting entities by amending specifications to reflect changes in building methods.

Maintenance of the continued relevance of any index requires the implementation on an on-going index review process. Elements of the process for construction price indices include:

- *Review of the composition of the list of projects:* Entails an examination of the list of model construction projects to ensure that they continue to be representative (e.g. use of new styles, size, etc.).

- *Review of the projects themselves:* Entails a review of individual projects within the list of model construction projects to ensure that the data item components (and their weights) reflect changes in technical standards, new construction methods, new building materials, etc.

- *Review of specifications:* To ensure they use current terminology, etc.

- *Review of respondent organisations:* To ensure that price data continue to be obtained from organisations representative of whole construction branch (e.g. a representative selection of large/small, government/non-government organisations).

Index Formulae

The formulae most commonly used in the compilation of construction price indices by OECD and European Union Member countries are the fixed base-weighted Laspeyres and the current-weighted Paasche.

Just over forty of the indices described use a Laspeyres formula, and a further five (in Belgium, and Canada) use chain Laspeyres (where the weights are updated annually). Seven of the indices described (in France, Sweden, and the United Kingdom) use the Paasche formula, whilst Australia uses elements of both fixed and current weighting in some of their construction price indices.

In Japan, indices for individual items that make up their construction price index are calculated as a Fisher Approximate Value, derived by combining the Laspeyres index with an approximate Paasche index.

Frequency of Compilation/Publication

Almost all of the construction price indices compiled by OECD and European Union Member countries are compiled and published either monthly or quarterly. The Belgian composite construction index is compiled annually, as are some of the Canadian indices. Two countries (Canada, and Luxembourg) compile construction price indices twice-yearly.

Some countries also produce more detailed special purpose indices (covering for example more detailed type of construction activity, trade groups, material components, regional disaggregations, etc.) on request.

A.   EXPLANATORY NOTES

Most OECD and European Union Member countries publish construction price indices that mainly differ from each other by the type and purpose of the index, construction activity coverage, and the items included in the compilation of the index. The descriptions of the country indices presented below are organised in three parts according to the three types of construction price indices described in Section 1B of this publication:

- input construction price indices compiled by 19 Member countries;

- output construction price indices compiled by 14 Member countries; and

- seller's price indices compiled by 3 Member countries.

The descriptions of these three types of indices presented below have, as far as possible, the following structure for each country.

In order to illustrate certain aspects of the concepts and compilation practices described in Sections 1 and 2 of this publication, more detailed descriptions are provided within some of the following sections for some countries.

Resume

Provides a brief overview of the construction price indices compiled in the country, and includes the title, main characteristics of the indices, method of compilation, and the name of the organisation primarily responsible for the compilation of the index.

Organisation responsible for index

The address of the organisation responsible for the compilation of the indices is given as a contact point for those wishing to access the index series, or requiring further information concerning the methodology used in its compilation.

Telephone and fax numbers

Correspond as far as possible to the service responsible for the compilation of the indices within the above organisation.

Other organisation involved

In some countries, organisations other than the primary organisation referred to above are involved in the compilation of the indices. These could be the national bank, relevant ministries, and other government agencies involved in housing policy, or the planning of civil engineering infrastructure work. These organisations may collect relevant price information or weights for their own needs. These elements may then be used by the primary organisation responsible for the compilation of the price indices.

Reference population

Describes the reporting units and the elements for which prices are observed. Reporting units include construction enterprises, materials suppliers, government organisations, etc. The observed elements correspond to the basket of items for which prices are monitored in the compilation of a PPI. They can be standard categories of construction works, input factors, etc.

Types of construction covered

Describes the type(s) of construction activity included in the indices. Often separate indices are compiled for different types of construction.

Geographic area covered

In some countries the indices apply to a limited area of the national territory (e.g. capital city, urban area, major cities), or are provided by region.

Items included in the indices

Describes the components included in the prices monitored for the indices. The components may be the cost of input factors such as materials, labour, profits, margins, productivity, overheads, VAT, cost of land, architects fees, etc. The inclusion or exclusion of these components determine the type of index compiled (input, output, seller's price).

Sources of data

Construction price indices are often compiled using information from a number of sources. These range from "raw" data obtained directly from construction enterprises, to the use of indices compiled for other purposes.

Method of compilation

Provides a limited description of the methodology used in the compilation of the index. For each index, this part refers to the typology described in Section 1C of this publication.

Compilation of weights

Describes the procedures used to compile the weights used in the indices.

Type of index, base year and frequency of compilation

Describes the main characteristics of the construction price indices compiled in the country: formula (Laspeyres, Paasche, etc.), base year, and frequency of compilation.

Use(s) of the index

Outlines the main uses of the indices described.

Publications

Gives an overview of the data available, and lists publications and other dissemination media where the index series are presented.

Where available, methodological references are also provided.

B.   INPUT CONSTRUCTION PRICE INDICES

AUSTRALIA

Resume

The Australian Bureau of Statistics (ABS) compiles price indices based on input costs covering civil engineering works. The Bureau also compiles three output price indices for: the construction and renovation of houses; construction of other dwellings; and construction of other buildings. These are described in this publication under Output Price Indices.

Organisation responsible for index

Australian Bureau of Statistics
PO Box 10
Belconnen, ACT 2616
Australia

Telephone and fax numbers

Tel: (+616) 252 6808

Fax: (+616) 252 5327

Types of construction covered

The index includes major civil engineering projects classified according to purpose, e.g. roads, communication facilities, etc.

Geographic area covered

The index is compiled for each of the eight States and Territories in Australia.

Items included in the indices

The price indices for civil engineering works are based on input costs comprising: materials (excluding the cost of transport to site), labour, and equipment hire. No taxes are included in these costs, which reflect any discounts available.

Sources of data

A periodic collection is undertaken (most recently in 1985), to determine the composition of expenditure for a number of State and Commonwealth public sector authorities on major construction projects. The expenditures are classified according to the purpose of the construction projects e.g. roads, communication facilities.

The cost information for materials and equipment hire is obtained from producer price index and foreign trade price index sources, together with some specially constructed indices, for example, road building activity. Labour costs are based on the system of pay awards, which set the legal minimum pay for each classification within an occupation. Social contributions paid by employers are not included.

Method of compilation

The indices are compiled using the standard factors method. A number of fixed-weighted input-cost indices are derived for various purpose categories of expenditure. The fixed weights are derived from information collected from various authorities on the composition of expenditure.

Compilation of weights

The periodic data collection referred to above is used in the selection and determination of weights for the 80 most significant expenditure items. Although this data collection is restricted to the public sector, the composition of expenditures for each purpose is considered to closely reflect the composition in the private sector.

The indices used for deflation in the national accounts have elements of fixed and current weighting. Fixed weighted price indices are derived for a number of purpose categories of expenditure. These purpose-based deflators are

39

current-weighted together using information on the value of work done by purpose from a quarterly engineering construction activity survey.

Type of index, base year and frequency of compilation

They are quarterly indices, with reference period July 1989 - June 1990 = 100.

Data for the index are collected quarterly.

Use(s) of index

The indices are used for deflation of corresponding aggregates in the Australian national accounts.

The indices are also used to derive quarterly constant price estimates of approvals, commencements, completion, and value of work done on engineering construction in Australia in total.

Publications

The index results are not published separately but are consistent with the total implicit price deflator for non-dwelling building, and construction as published quarterly in *Australian National Accounts: National Income, Expenditure and Product* (ABS Cat. No. 5206.0) and the *State Accounts* (ABS Cat. No. 5242.0). Separate indices for construction activity by State and Territory and for some purpose categories of expenditure are available on request.

Resume

The Austrian Central Statistical Office (ÖSTAT) calculates two factor costs indices for the construction sector: the monthly housing and estate building costs index (1990=100), and the monthly construction cost index for road and bridge construction (1990=100) described below.

The indices are compiled using the standard factors method.

ÖSTAT also compiles five output price indices covering the whole construction sector. These are described in this publication under Output Price Indices.

Organisation responsible for index

Österreichisches Statistisches Zentralamt (ÖSTAT)
Abteilung 3: Produktion und Dienstleistungen
Hintere Zollamtstraße 2b,
A - 1033 WIEN

Telephone and fax numbers

Tel: (+431) 711 28 7065

Fax: (+431) 715 68 29

Other organisation involved

Until the end of the 1980s, an index of changes in building costs was calculated by the Ministry for Economic Affairs. This was in addition to the indices compiled by the Federal Building Industry Association (Bundesinnung der Baugewerbe). After the 1980s the Ministry handed over responsibility for the calculation of a harmonised system of building factor cost indices to the Central Statistical Office (ÖSTAT).

Reference population

Prices are collected for a basket of components based on six specimen projects (two versions for each of: a single-family house; a terraced house; and a multi-storey apartment building). The price of each component, belonging either to wage costs or to other costs, is determined in reference to a typical building, a combination of the three types of buildings listed above, weighted on the basis of the results of 1986-87 ÖSTAT housing construction statistics.

Types of construction covered

The index is calculated for residential buildings, road construction, and bridge construction.

The housing and estate building costs index: Covers only residential buildings, and is based on three types of building: single-family houses; terraced houses; and multi-storey apartment buildings.

The costs are determined for building works carried out by the contractor and other trades such as electricians or plumbers. They cover standard site preparation, main building activities, joinery, painting and sanitary installations (parts of NACE Rev.1 groups 45.1, 45.2, 45.3 and 45.4). Parts of building installation and completion (groups 45.3 and 45.4) and furniture are not covered.

In addition, some service activities are included in the index. These include costs of design, tendering, stress analysis, preparation of applications and work schedule, site supervision. Costs of land, site development, costs for special foundations are not covered.

The road construction cost index: Covers only road construction.

The bridge construction cost index: Covers only bridge construction.

Geographic area covered

The price indices refer only to projects undertaken in Austria.

Items included

The housing and estate building costs indices: Show the evolution of the costs of construction of residential buildings from the enterprise point of view. They are measured as a weighted average of the prices of two input factors needed to construct a building: labour and materials. It does not include productivity, margins, and taxes linked to construction activity.

Sources of data

Data for the factor prices indices are obtained from the following sources:

- industrial wholesale price index

- wages structural survey

- collective agreements

- social insurance costs (provided by Bundesinnung der Baugewerbe).

Compilation of weights

The housing and estate building costs index: Uses weights based on 1986-87 housing construction statistics, and refers to the components needed to build a theoretical building that is a combination of three typical buildings. The components are weighted as follows:

- "wages costs": 52.94 %

comprising:

Contractor	27.94%
Auxiliary and related trades	13.84%
Metalworking and electrical installation	11.16%

- "other costs": 47.06%

comprising 39 products that are each weighted as for example:

Wooden joinery	6.23%
Diesel	0.74%
Paint	0.40%
etc.	

The road construction costs index: The total weight of the wages component is 34.8 per cent, and is taken from the contractor's work component in the housing and estate building costs index. Many of the products are taken from the basket of the wholesale price index. Imported bitumen is taken from foreign trade statistics.

The total weight of the "other" component is 65.2 per cent.

Weights are available for total cost factors (wages, and other) and function groups (earthworks and superstructure, drainage and permanent support systems, asphalt work). These are further broken down by individual functions (e.g. depreciation and interest, repair steel, gravel, concrete etc.).

The bridge construction costs index: Uses weights obtained from the same sources as the road construction index. Weights are available for total cost factors (wages, and other), materials groups and individual products.

Type of index, base year and frequency of compilation

The housing and estate building costs indices: Are calculated according to a Laspeyres formula. The wages costs component is a weighted average of the:

- contractor's wage component;

- auxiliary and related trades wage component;

- wage component for electrical installations and metalworking.

The contractor's wage component is obtained on the basis of the collectively agreed wage (CAW) for the building industry. The average hourly wage (AHW) is calculated in accordance with

ÖSTAT wage structure surveys, levelled out on the basis of the average overpayment factor (ratio of AHW and CAW).

The auxiliary and related trades wage component correspond to the collective agreement for the carpenter master trade.

The wage component for electrical installations and metal working is derived from the:

- collective agreement the iron and metal producing and manufacturing industry (for 46 per cent of the value); and the

- collective agreement for the iron and metal working trade (for 54 per cent of the value).

The other costs component is calculated on the basis of the weighted figure for paint from the consumers price index and the weighted figures for the products represented in the wholesale price index.

The price basis for the components is the annual average of 1990. Since the January 1990 reference month, the index of building costs for housing construction, previously known as the Maculan Index, has not been published, and has been replaced by the new housing and estate construction costs index calculated by ÖSTAT. The two index series may be linked by applying factors linking them to the official housing and estate costs index (1990=100).

The road construction costs; and bridge construction indices: Are calculated according to a Laspeyres formula. The wages component, available only on a yearly basis for the civil engineering sector, is taken from the housing and estate building costs index. The other component is largely calculated from the figures for the products represented in the wholesale price index, except for the electricity component taken from the consumer price index.

The base year for the weights of the "other" component for the civil engineering indices is 1983.

All three indices are calculated monthly.

Publications

The three indices are published separately for residential building, bridge construction, and road construction.

The housing and estate building costs index: Are published monthly in the form of rapid reports, broken down by overall building costs (total, wages, other), and contractor costs (total, wages, other) in *Statistische Nachrichten* (Annex: *Statistische Übersichten*, Table 2.1; conversion with Vol.3/1991), and stored in the ÖSTAT ISIS database.

The road construction costs; and the bridge construction indices: Are published monthly in the form of rapid reports, broken down by overall construction costs (total, wages, other), the other component being broken down by cost groups, and the group indices "asphalt and surfacing work" being broken down by origin of bitumen.

It is published in the publication *Statistische Nachrichten* (Annex: *Statistische Übersichten*, Table 2.1) on a monthly basis since January 1992, and stored in the ÖSTAT ISIS database.

Resume

The Belgian National Institute of Statistics calculates a yearly construction factor prices index based on the costs of the labour and materials inputs to the construction sector.

It aims to cover the whole field of construction: new construction, and renovation of residential buildings (both public and private); non-residential buildings; and civil engineering.

Organisation responsible for index

Institut National de Statistiques /
Nationaal Instituut voor de Statistiek
Rue de Louvain, 44
B-1000 BRUXELLES

Telephone and fax numbers

Tel: (+32) 2 548 6571

Fax: (+32) 2 548 6254

Types of construction covered

The index aims to cover the whole field of construction: new construction, and renovation of residential buildings (both public and private); non-residential buildings; and civil engineering.

The materials selected for the construction price index accounted for 68 per cent of the sector's total inputs in 1980, and belong to nine different NACE groups.

Geographic area covered

The index covers the whole of Belgium.

Items included

The index is based on the costs of labour and materials. Costs of the transport of materials, equipment hire, installation costs, professional fees, profits, etc. are not covered in the index.

The labour costs data are obtained from statistics on gross hourly earnings in the building construction industry, as compiled by the National Institute of Statistics. For this exercise mid-year figures are estimated as an average of the April and October figures. The earnings data do not include social contributions paid by employers.

The costs used exclude taxes, and include any discounts that apply.

Sources of data

The data on material costs are obtained from the national index of prices of domestic industrial production.

Type of index, base year and frequency of compilation

The index is calculated annually, according to the chain Laspeyres method and has base period 1985=100.

In constructing the index, materials and wages are given equal weight.

Publications

The index results are not published, but are used in the conversion to current prices of the buildings element within gross fixed capital formation of the national accounts.

Resume

Seven construction price indices are calculated in Canada. These comprise four input, two output, and one seller's price indices. The four input indices described below cover:

- Residential/non-residential building input prices
- Electric utility construction
- Telecommunications plant
- Construction union wage rates

The sellers price index, and the four input price indices are described in this publication under Output Price Indices and Seller's Price Indices.

No aggregate index combining the seven separate construction price indices is compiled.

Organisation Responsible for Index

Statistics Canada
Jean Talon Building
Tunney's Pasture
Ottawa, Ontario
Canada KIA OT6

Telephone and fax numbers

Tel: (+613) 951 9615

Fax: (+613) 951 2848

Types of construction covered

Residential/non-residential building input prices: Are monthly indices of input prices, covering both private residential building, and non-residential building.

Electric utility construction: Measure price change for the construction of five separate models of electrical utility plant. These indices are compiled biannually. They are based mainly on the prices of inputs to the construction of electric utilities. At present they are restricted to new construction, but may in future be extended to major renovation and refurbishment projects.

The models relate to: distribution systems; transmission lines; transformer stations; hydro-electric generating stations; and fossil-fuel fired generating stations.

Telecommunications plant: Measure price changes through time for annual capital expenditures of the Canadian telecommunications industry. These indices, which are calculated annually, reflect purchase price changes between consecutive years for a matched sample of goods.

Construction union wage rates: These monthly indices cover wage rates for the unionised construction labour trades. They measure changes over time in the current collective agreement rates for 16 trades engaged in building construction in 22 metropolitan areas. Thus they cover trades working in all branches of construction activity.

Geographic area covered

Electric utility construction: All Canada.

Telecommunications plant: All Canada.

Construction union wage rates: Indices are provided for those cities where a majority of trades are covered by current collective agreements.

Items included in the indices

Residential/non-residential building input prices: The items covered in these input price indices are restricted to the cost of materials (but not their transport to the site) and the cost of unionised labour. For residential construction 37 material items are costed, while 46 are costed for non-residential construction. For costing purposes the labour inputs are broken down into 16 trades.

No taxes are included in the cost figures used, nor are any discounts reflected. The labour costs data do not include social contributions paid by employers.

Electric utility construction: Each model portrays an average mix of inputs from a variety of projects in a specific base period. The elements included in the indices are materials (including their transport to the site), equipment hire, labour, land preparation costs, architects' and engineers' fees, major machinery elements and equipment components (e.g. turbine generators, power boilers, power transformers, tanks), overheads and profits.

Sales taxes are included where known. The prices do not reflect discounts.

Telecommunications plant: Elements included in the indices are materials (including their transportation to the site), equipment hire, labour, land preparation costs, permits, installation costs where applicable, engineers' fees, overheads and profits. The prices include provincial sales taxes. They are net of discounts.

Construction union wage rates: These are indices of wage rates. Two rates are indexed: basic rates, indicating the straight time hourly compensation; and basic rates including supplements, such as vacation pay, statutory holiday pay and employers' contribution to pension plans, health and welfare plans, industry promotion and training funds.

Sources of data

Residential/non-residential building input prices: For these indices the data for the monthly calculations are obtained from producer price index sources, and, for labour costs, on the basis of rates set in collective wage agreements.

Electric utility construction: The sources used for the indices include purchase data relating to the electric utilities, and consumer and producer price index data. The sample for the purchase data covers 10-12 companies.

The labour costs data are obtained from surveys of employers as well as from information on collective wage agreements. They do not include social contributions paid by employers.

A large number of items, varying between 100 and 200 according to the type of project, are costed for the indices. They are selected from an analysis of completed projects data so as to cover 70 per cent of total project direct costs.

Telecommunications plant: The data used in construction of these indices are primarily drawn from purchasers' records of participating telecommunications companies (or carriers).

Construction union wage rates: These indices are based on signed collective wage agreements, and are obtained with the collaboration of the Canadian Construction Association and the local (city) Construction Labour Relations Associations (employers groups), and in some cases, provincial government bodies.

Method of compilation

Electric utility construction: Each of the five models was developed after extensive consultation with major Canadian electric utilities and the Canadian Electrical Association.

Telecommunications plant: Each participating company, following a set of guidelines, constructs annual price indices appropriate to their gross additions to capital stock. The national totals published by Statistics Canada are aggregates of these carrier indices. The carrier indices are based on current reproduction cost, i.e. the cost of acquiring assets in a given period identical to those placed in service during a comparison period. These are based on costs of materials, wages and other inputs.

Compilation of weights

Residential/non-residential building input prices: For residential construction the index weights are based on a survey of building contractors which was undertaken in the late 1960s. It is planned to repeat this survey to update the weights in the mid-1990s. For non-residential construction the weights are based on analysis of input-output tables.

Electric utility construction: The present weights used in the indices are based on information from surveys, stratified by type of utility plant, covering (approximately) the years 1965-73 and about 15 per cent of total construction output in this sector.

Telecommunications plant: The purchase weights estimates come from an annual survey of the values of gross additions by carriers related to the previous calendar year.

Type of index, base year and frequency of compilation

The residential/non-residential building input prices; electric utility construction; and construction union wage rates indices are calculated according to the Laspeyres formula.

The telecommunications plant indices are calculated according to the chain Laspeyres formula.

The residential/non-residential building input prices indices have a reference base year of 1981=100.

The other three indices have a base year of 1986=100 (there are also plans to change this to 1992).

Electric utility construction: These indices are compiled biannually.

Telecommunications plant: Are compiled annually.

Construction union wage rates: Are compiled monthly.

Use(s) of index

These indices are used for a variety of purposes, e.g. analysing price change in construction and fixed capital formation, deflating components of the national accounts, for contract escalation, and for estimates of reproduction cost, either for recosting budgets or for revaluing fixed assets.

Publications

Residential/non-residential building input prices: These indices are not published, but are used for output and final expenditure deflation, contract escalation, and insurance purposes. In addition to the aggregate results separate indices are calculated for materials and labour costs, by trade groups (architectural, structural, mechanical, and electrical), and by regions (Atlantic, Quebec, Ontario, Prairies, British Columbia).

Electric utility construction: The indices are first published in Statistics Canada's *The Daily* (Cat. No. 11-001E). They are also published biannually in *Construction Price Statistics* (Cat. No.62-007). As well as the overall index, indices are also available by construction model components and by broad asset categories (transmission lines, transformer stations, distribution systems, generation facilities - steam, hydro, nuclear). Data are available only at national level.

Telecommunications plant: The indices are first released in Statistics Canada's *The Daily* (Cat. No. 11-001E). They are also published annually *in Construction Price Statistics* (Cat. No. 62-007). As well as the overall index, separate indices are also available by major asset categories (outside plant, central office equipment, station equipment, general equipment). Data are available only at national level.

Construction union wage rates: The indices are first released in Statistics Canada's *The Daily* (Cat. No. 11-001E). They are also published monthly in the *Daily Bulletin*, and are available in *Construction Price Statistics* (Cat. No. 62-007). Indices are available for basic rates and for basic rates including supplements. As well as the overall indices, separate indices are available by trade and trade group (architectural, structural, mechanical, electrical), and by city. Indices are available for 22 metropolitan cities in Canada.

DENMARK

Resume

Denmark Statistics calculates two sets of input price indices:

- the regulating price index for residential building,
- the regulating price index for civil engineering.

The regulating price index for residential construction: Was created in January 1987 and first published in May 1989 to replace two previous construction costs indices covering respectively, the one-family houses, and the multi-dwellings buildings of prefabricated design. They take account of the materials and labour costs.

The indices are compiled using the standard factors method on the basis of weights corresponding to a specific building project constructed in 1987.

The regulating price indices were created on the initiative of the Ministry of Construction and take into account the major changes that had occurred in the techniques and materials used by the construction industry since the 1960s. The new indices no longer distinguish between one family houses and multiple dwellings buildings because the techniques and materials used for the construction of these two types of buildings have become more similar. The number of prefabricated houses has increased and more and more buildings are built with different technical characteristics. In addition, the weighting scheme had to be revised because part of the materials and techniques used in its compilation were not used anymore.

The current weighting scheme dates back from January 1987 and should be revised at least every 10 years.

The input price indices for civil engineering works: Comprise a set of six indices originally established at the request of the Road Directorate in the Ministry of Transports to serve as a basis for the estimation of the cost of road construction. Later on, the indices were also used by building contractors as benchmarks for the escalation of contracts for other civil engineering works.

The first group of indices was first calculated in 1959 and relate to main road, and motorway works. The second group of indices was first calculated in 1976 and relate to earth works, surface asphalt works, concrete structures (bridges of concrete), and iron structures (iron bridges).

In March 1996, the two indices of the first group were merged into one under the name "cost index for road building", and all indices were rebated to 1995=100.

The indices are currently compiled using the standard factors method on the basis of weights agreed upon by several organisations involved in the construction sector.

Organisation responsible for index

Denmark's Statistik
Sejrøgade, 11
Postboks 2550
DK - 2100 KØBENHAVN Ø

Telephone and fax numbers

Tel.(+45) 39 17 39 17

Fax. (+45) 31 18 48 01

Types of construction covered

Regulating price index for residential building: Covers main building works, building installation and completion for new residential buildings. Site preparation activities are not covered by the index.

Data are broken down according to ten professions and to a classification of seven elements of the building structure (type of work). Each category of building work is supplied by one or more professions. Each profession is responsible for several standard building operations.

Indices are calculated for the breakdowns by profession and element of building structure, for materials and labour costs separately and as a whole.

In addition to these breakdowns, special indices are compiled for glaziers carried out as a separate contract; and for heavy concrete structures.

The indices are not calculated according to the NACE (i.e. in terms of NACE Rev.1 activities, groups 45.2, 45.3 and 45.4), but according to a specific classification by profession and by categories of building works.

Regulating price index for civil engineering: Covers the new construction of six types of works: main road works, motorway works, earth works, surfacing and asphalt works, concrete works, iron works.

Denmark Statistics plan to calculate additional indices for the repair and maintenance of roads, and specific indices for individual extraordinary projects, such as the bridge that will be built between Denmark and Sweden.

Geographic area covered

The costs surveyors are situated in different parts of Denmark, and the indices compiled cover the whole country (excluding Greenland).

Items included

Regulating price index for residential building: The material prices are calculated on the basis of list prices or producer prices excluding general discounts such as quantity discounts, function discounts that relate only to materials such as concrete, stone or wood. Cash discounts are not deducted.

The labour costs are calculated on the basis of collective agreement wages, plus compulsory employers contributions, minus subsidies to employers for the payment of these contributions.

Profits, fees, VAT and employers payment of employee's first and second days of unemployment are not included in the index.

The cost of land is not included in the index.

Regulating price index for civil engineering: The prices of materials are based on wholesale prices received by the producers of the input materials.

They include import duties and exclude VAT and special taxes. Cash reductions are not taken into account.

The labour costs are limited to hours actually worked and are based on labour market agreements. They include social contributions. They exclude prepayment of wages and salaries, expenses for expropriation and administrative costs, except for the building of motor ways, for which administrative costs and planning costs are included.

The hire of equipment includes the operators.

Sources of data

Regulating price index for residential building: Data are obtained from ten professional cost surveyors and eight manufacturers of concrete structures.

Regulating price index for civil engineering: Data for materials are obtained from producer price indices produced by Denmark Statistics. Data for labour costs are based on labour agreements for Nord-Seeland, zone 1 and 2, plus the area outside the Capital City area.

The basis of prices for hire costs is the current price rates provided for the Danish Haulage Contractors Union.

Method of compilation

Regulating price index for residential building: Data are collected for:

* prices of specific materials and specific quantities,
* collective agreements on wages and supplements to wages, and
* social contributions paid by the employer.

The index is compiled using the standard factors method on the basis of weights corresponding to a specific building project constructed in 1987.

Regulating price index for civil engineering: Data are collected for:

- prices of a sample of representative materials,
- collective agreements on wages and supplements to wages, and
- equipment hire with operator.

The index is compiled using the standard factors method on the basis of weights agreed upon by several organisations involved in the construction sector.

Compilation of weights

Regulating price index for residential building: The weighting system refers to a specific building project (called Mölholm) that was characterised by a group of one-storey or two-storey terraced houses with 2 to 6 flats in each building, each with an average net floor space area of 81 square metres per flat.

For each category of building work the share of each cost component (material or labour) is defined according to the shares observed for this given construction project. In the same way, the weights attached to each category of building works for the calculation of the total index, were observed on the Mölholm project in January 1987.

Regulating price index for civil engineering: The aggregations are based on weights agreed upon by the Road Directorate of the Ministry of Transport, the railways company, the Union of Contractors, and Denmark Statistics.

The weights are based on standard constructions for civil engineering projects including sub-contractors.

Type of index, base year and frequency of compilation

Both indices are calculated on a quarterly basis according to a fixed weight Laspeyres formula.

Regulating price index for residential building: The base year used for the calculation of the index is 1987.

Regulating price index for civil engineering: Since March 1996, all these indices are calculated according to the base year 1995=100.

Use(s) of the index

The indices are used for national accounts deflation.

Publications

The indices are broken down into sub-indices on materials and labour costs according to the total, the category of building work, and by profession.

The regulating price indices are published in:

- Statistiske Efterretninger (Statistical News)
- *Nyt fra Denmark's Statistik* (News from Denmark Statistics)
- *Statistisk årbog* (Statistical Yearbook)
- *Prisstatistik* (Price Statistics)
- *Statistisk tiårsoversigt* (Statistical Ten-years Review)
- DSTB (time-series database)

Further details on the methodology of the indices can be found in *Bygge- og anlægsvirksomhed*, No.°14, 1989 (Construction Industry) in the series *Statistiske Efterretninger* (Statistical News).

Resume

Statistics Finland produces the "index of building costs", a composite index compiled from a set of monthly input price indices based on standard factor costs.

The indices cover new construction, both public and private sector, of five main building types.

In addition, there is a renovation index common to all building types.

Organisation responsible for index

Statistics Finland
Työpajakatu 13
FN - Helsinki.

Telephone and fax numbers

Tel: (+358) 0 1734 2238

Fax: (+358) 0 1734 3429

Types of construction covered

The indices cover new public and private sector construction of five main building types:

- single-unit residential buildings
- blocks of flats
- office and commercial buildings
- warehouses and production buildings
- buildings used in agricultural production.

In addition, there is a renovation index common to all building types.

Items included

All published indices are calculated using the same nomenclature of inputs. Ninety five cost items are defined.

The indices show the average level of building costs in the whole country at the moment of observation in relation to the level in the base year for a structurally identical building constructed using the same methods as in the base year.

The indices include a wide range of cost items: materials (including their transport to site), labour, equipment hire, site preparation costs, conveyancing and professional fees, installation and fitting costs, interest on loans and trade margins.

The "building cost index for residential construction" includes value added tax as a cost component. Otherwise, the indices do not include VAT. Prices are net of discounts.

The salaries data are based on salaries actually paid per hour worked, rather than collective agreements. The data on labour costs include social contributions paid by employers.

Sources of data

A wide range of sources are used to obtain the cost data for the indices. These include both construction and other enterprises, price lists, producer price index data and, in the case of oil and electricity, producers associations.

The data on labour costs are taken from the wages statistics of the Confederation of Finnish Industry and Employers.

Method of compilation

The indices measure the level of building costs with the help of trends in the prices of the basic inputs used (labour, materials and services). Each input influences the overall index in proportion to its share in building budgets (unit price multiplied by quantity used) in the base year.

The prices of 95 representative items that are monitored for the indices, together with the related weights, were selected by the Laboratory for Building Economy of the Technical Research Centre of Finland from an examination of five typical buildings, one for each of the building types covered in the indices.

Corrections are applied to take account of delays in obtaining data, and a 12 month moving average is used to avoid seasonal fluctuations.

Compilation of weights

The weights were determined according to each item's share of total construction cost in the base year.

The weightings are reviewed every 5 to 10 years, along with the selection of factors included in the indices.

Type of index, base year and frequency of compilation

The indices are compiled monthly according to the Laspeyres formula and relate to the base year 1990=100.

Publications

Data series: As well as aggregate indices, a variety of separate indices are published, for materials and labour costs, by trade, and by product nomenclature.

The indices are published monthly in *Rakennuskustannusindeksi.* Statistics Finland can also calculate other indices corresponding to clients' needs, within the limits set by the raw data available and considerations of data confidentiality.

In addition to the cost variables of the index of building costs, sub-indices of the producer price indices (e.g. index of wholesale prices and index of import prices) are also available.

Methodology: The structure and principles of the index are explained in more detail in *Rakennuskustannusindeksi 1990=100*, produced (in Finnish and English) by the construction laboratory of the State Technical Research Institute, and Statistics Finland. This is published by Rakentajain Kustannus Oy.

FRANCE

Resume

The International and Economic Affairs Directorate of the Ministry of Equipment and Housing (Direction des Affaires Economiques et Internationales du Ministère de l'Equipement et du Logement -- DAEI) compiles monthly input price indices for the building construction sector (BT) based on the factors costs. Fifty indices represent specialised types of works, and one index (BT01) represents the whole building industry.

The BT indices were created for construction contract escalation purposes. They are normally used when the work commences long after the building contract was signed, or when construction takes place over a long period. They apply to both private and public sector contracts.

The Ministry of Economic Affairs calculates similar input price indices for the civil engineering sector (TP). Twenty five indices represent the specialised types of works, and one index (TP01) represents the whole civil engineering industry.

These indices are used for national account deflation.

The indices are compiled using the standard factors method on the basis of weights last revised in 1991.

An output price index is also compiled in France. This is described in this publication under Output Price Indices.

Organisation responsible for index

Ministère de l'Equipement et du Logement
Direction des Affaires Economiques
 et Internationales
Tour Pascal B
F-92055 Paris-La-Défense Cedex 04

Telephone and fax numbers

Tel: (+33) 1 40 81 26 81

Fax: (+33) 1 40 81 26 99

Other organisation involved

The BT indices are compiled by the DAEI on the basis of formulae defined in collaboration with the National Building Federation (Fédération Nationale du Bâtiment), trade unions, and professional associations of the construction sector, and on notice of the Prices Commission (Commission des Prix).

TP indices are compiled using precise weights of different factor price indices defined by the Direction Générale de la Concurrence, de la Consommation et de la Répression des Fraudes (DGCCRF) of the Ministry of Economy (the general directorate responsible for controlling the competition and consumer market conditions and tax evasion) after consultation with the Fédération Nationale des Travaux Publics (FNTP) (national professional association for the civil engineering sector), at the direction of the consultative commission on prices of materials (COCIM).

By law, the weights for both BT and TP indices are published in the *Bulletin Officiel - Concurrence, Consommation, Répression des Fraudes* (BOCCRF).

Types of construction covered

BT indices: Are calculated for 50 types of construction works such as site preparation (BT02), tiling (BT09), ventilation and air conditioning (BT41), repair and maintenance (BT50).

The indices only cover the building industry, and refer to a nomenclature of types construction of works covering parts of NACE Rev.1 groups 45.1 (site preparation), 45.2 (complete constructions or parts of thereof), 45.3 (building installation), and 45.4 (building completion).

TP indices: Are calculated for 13 types of works such as general earth moving (TP03), sea and river dredging (TP06), electrification networks with equipment (TP12), metal frames and structures (TP13).

Cover only the civil engineering industry, and refer to a nomenclature of types of works covering part of NACE Rev.1 groups 45.1, 45.2 and 45.5 (renting of construction or demolition equipment with operator).

Geographic area covered

The price indices used in the composition of the index all refer to French domestic prices.

Items included

BT indices: Show the evolution of the costs of construction in the building sector measured as a weighted average of the prices of the different input factors needed to construct a building. These include labour, materials, transports, equipment, energy and general expenses. It doesn't include productivity, margins and taxes linked to construction activity. Architect fees and price of land are also excluded.

For a given index (type of construction work), the costs can change according to three factors:

- rises in the prices of the input factors (labour, materials, equipment),
- changes in the quantities of input factors needed to obtain the same result, and
- quality changes in the input factors.

The BT indices are only meant to measure the influence of the first factor, that is changes in the price of the input factors. The effects of quantity and quality changes are removed.

TP indices: Show the evolution of the costs of construction in the civil engineering sector measured as a weighted average of the prices of the different input factors needed to carry out a civil engineering project. These include labour, materials, equipment, energy and general expenses. It doesn't include productivity and margins linked to the construction activity. Architect fees and price of land are also excluded.

Sources of data

Each input price index is defined in terms of the percentage of each component participating in the total cost of the construction project. A price index calculated by different authorities is attached to each component. The components are:

- *Salaries:* general index of salaries in the building and civil engineering sector published in the FNB.

- *Expenses:* percentage of social expenses according to salaries.

- *Materials:* part of the materials indices are published in the BOCCRF (cement, bricks, tiles, plaster, iron and steel materials, etc.). Indices for the other materials are compiled from lists of prices published by producers or professional associations.

- *Equipment:* index of equipment prices calculated by INSEE.

- *Transport:* special index of road transport cost compiled by the DAEI together with professional associations. It corresponds to the weighted sum of a labour cost index (0.4), the producer price index for transport vehicles (0.35), the consumer price index for diesel oil (0.2) and the producer price index for the manufacture of rubber tyres and tubes (0.05). These indices are published by INSEE.

- *Energy:* the energy consumed for a construction is multiplied by the consumption price index for diesel oil published by INSEE.

- *Other expenses:* this component includes:

  · 21% of building renting expenses (ICC index - Construction Output Price Index -- from *Journal Officiel*);

  · 16% of office and accounting paper supplies (INSEE);

  · 21% of communication expenses (INSEE);

  · 13% of other use of vehicles expenses (INSEE);

  · 14% of transport services (INSEE);

· 5% of office machinery (PCs and printers) (INSEE); and

· 5% engineering.

The percentages of each component forming the structure for each index is published in the BOCCRF.

Method of compilation

The indices are compiled using the standard factors method.

The elements of the component indices are mainly obtained from existing indices published by different institutions such as INSEE, other Ministries, national federation of building, national federation of civil engineering, trade associations, etc..

However, except for a number of basic materials (cement, bricks, tiles, plaster, iron and steel products), there are no official material price indices. The DAEI and the FNB conduct two simultaneous monthly surveys to collect 425 price materials from 96 suppliers. The results of the surveys are confronted at the end of each month and the resulting price indices are incorporated in the index.

Compilation of weights

Each index corresponds to a category of building work. For each index a structure is defined in terms of percentages of input factors necessary to carry out the construction project. These structures can differ dramatically from one index to the other. For instance, the respective structures for the indices BT02 (site preparation), BT04 (brickwork), BT46 (painting) and BT01 (all building works) are:

Component item	BT02 %	BT04 %	BT46 %	BT01 %
Salaries and social expenses	36	46	58	43
Materials	0	31	27	32
Equipment	36	5	3	4
Transports	0	2	0	3
Energy	10	2	0	3
General expenses	18	14	12	15

For each index, the materials component item is broken down according to a specific list of materials for which the weights are also pre-defined. For instance, the materials used for the category of construction work "brickwork" (BT04) are bricks (16%), cement (3%), and insulation material (12%).

These very detailed weights were first defined in 1974, together with the definition and coding of the indices, and published in the official journal (on 26 May 1972). The last revision dates back to October 1991.

Type of index, base year and frequency of compilation

The BT and TP indices are calculated monthly.

The BT and TP indices are chained indices. They are calculated each month by applying to the preceding month index the growth rate between month m and month $m-1$ obtained from the prices of the current and preceding months.

They correspond to a weighted average of component indices (personnel, materials, transports, equipment, energy and general expenses). Each component index itself is a weighted average of element indices that are either official indices, or product price indices for the elementary products used in construction collected from a number of important suppliers of the construction industry.

The composition of each component index is outlined above in "Sources of Data".

The BT indices are chained starting from the base year 1974.

The TP indices are chained starting from the base 100 corresponding to the economic conditions of January 1995.

Publications

BT indices: Are released monthly in Bulletin Officiel du Ministère de l'Equipement. The index BT01 is released monthly in Journal Officiel (JO) de la République Française

The TP indices: Are released monthly in Bulletin Officiel - Concurrence, Consommation, Répression des Fraudes.

GREECE

Resume

The National Statistical Service of Greece (NSSG) has calculated a price index for input materials for the construction of new residential buildings since 1971.

In 1980, this construction cost index was revised for the first time, and the NSSG decided to calculate a construction output price index also covering new residential building. This is described in this publication under Output Price Indices.

The last revision occurred in 1990, and a total price index of construction costs for new residential buildings is now compiled quarterly. It includes the costs of materials, as well as the labour costs and other expenditures.

The indices are compiled using the standard factors method on the basis of weights obtained from the accounting records of a number of construction contractors.

Three separate indices are available: cost of materials (monthly); labour costs (quarterly); and other expenditures (monthly).

Organisation responsible for index

National Statistical Service of Greece (NSSG)
14-16 Lycourgou Street
GR-10166 ATHENS

Telephone and fax numbers

Tel: (+30) 1 32 43 669/32 89 509

Fax: (+30) 1 32 23 159

Types of construction covered

The new buildings construction activities refer to a classification of materials in fifteen headings such as: plaster and concrete, natural stone material, plumbing, heating and sanitary ware of metal, electrical materials or fuels and lubricants for mechanical excavators and machinery.

The labour costs index refers to a classification of construction works such as: excavations, wall construction, central heating installations, insulation.

The compiled indices refer to a catalogue of selected materials and construction works.

Geographic area covered

The indices refer only to the buildings constructed in the Greater Athens area, but they can be considered as representative of all urban areas in the country.

Items included

The prices taken into account in the index refer to the prices paid by the constructor for the materials, the labour force and other expenditures.

The prices collected for the materials refer to prices actually paid by building enterprises for materials delivered at the work site, and they include transport and other expenses (VAT, etc.) charged by the purchaser. They all refer to transactions made during the reference month.

Labour costs refer to the prices actually paid to trade persons by the construction enterprises. Labour remuneration is usually agreed between the building enterprise and trade persons by speciality according to the volume of work, otherwise according to contract work (not according to wages). Use is made of contract prices collected quarterly, and refer to the agreements made during the quarter concerned.

Prices for the index of other expenditures are compiled monthly from competent organisations.

Sources of data

Data are collected through statistical surveys conducted by means of telephone enquiries and individual visits. The information is collected from the following reporting units that are selected according to the volume and value of their transactions:

- prices of materials obtained from commercial or industrial enterprises (suppliers),

- labour costs obtained from the contractors (construction enterprises), and

- other expenditures obtained from competent organisations.

Compilation of weights

The weighting coefficients were obtained from an analysis of the accounting records of 150 building enterprise for the period 1988 to 1990.

Type of index, base year and frequency of compilation

The index is calculated according to a Laspeyres formula and refers to base year 1990. It is calculated monthly for the prices of materials, and quarterly for the other components of the index.

Use(s) of the index

The index is used for statistical purposes such as deflation and in the compilation of national accounts.

Publications

The index is published in the Monthly Statistical Bulletin, the Statistical Yearbook of Greece, and in the Concise Statistical Yearbook.

ICELAND

Resume

Statistics Iceland calculates a monthly price index for construction using the standard factors method which is based on input costs.

Organisation responsible for index

Statistics Iceland
Skuggasundi 3
150 Reykjavik

Telephone and fax numbers

Tel: (+354) 560 9800

Fax: (+354) 562 8865

Types of construction covered

The coverage of the index is restricted to privately built apartments.

Items included in the indices

The elements included in the index are the cost of materials, including their transport to the site, labour, equipment hire, the cost of the leasing of land and its preparation, permits, fittings and installation costs, professional fees of architects and engineers, and overheads. The installation costs that are covered in the index comprise cold water supply, geothermal water supply for heating, and electricity.

The treatment of VAT is as follows. VAT on materials is included, but VAT on labour is excluded, because VAT paid on labour costs associated with residential building is refunded by the government. The prices used reflect discounts.

Sources of data

The price data used in the index are obtained from suppliers of building materials and from price lists. Around 1 700 to 1 800 price quotations are received each month.

The labour costs data are obtained from employers, and are partly based on the wage rates set in collective wage agreements and partly on wage surveys conducted twice a year in the construction industry. They include social contributions paid by employers.

Method of compilation

The items costed in the index were selected on the basis of cost analyses of finished residential building constructions. 429 items are costed for the index.

Type of index, base year and frequency of compilation

The index is compiled monthly according to the Laspeyres formula and has been newly rebated on January 1996=100. A feature of the recent rebasing and revision of the index was the change from the use of arithmetic average prices to geometric average prices.

Publications

The index results are published monthly in the statistical bulletin published by Statistics Iceland. In addition to aggregate results separate indices are provided for materials and labour costs and by trade.

Resume

Several cost or price indices for the construction sector are calculated in Ireland by different organisations according to their needs.

The Dublin Municipal Authority calculates a monthly house building cost index. This corresponds to a standard house built by the State. It applies to a limited area: the Capital City (Dublin).

This index is compiled using the standard factors method.

The Irish Central Statistical Office (CSO) calculates a monthly wholesale price index for building and construction materials. The CSO also calculates a capital goods price index, derived by combining a special hourly wage rate index with the wholesale price index mentioned above.

Organisation responsible for index

Central Statistics Office
Skehard Road
CORK

Telephone and fax numbers

Tel: (+353) 21 - 35 90 00 ext. 5547 or 5565

Fax: (+353) 21 - 35 91 65

Other organisation involved

The monthly index of house building cost is compiled by the Dublin Municipal Authority.

Reference population

House building cost index: The survey for this index follows the prices of a representative basket of materials used in the construction of a standard house in 1975, as well as the labour costs of skilled and unskilled workers involved in the construction of this house.

Wholesale prices index of materials: The reporting units for this index are the wholesalers, who report on all building materials combined, and for eleven separate categories of materials.

Types of construction covered

The classification used to identify "products" or materials in the construction sector is the Combined Nomenclature [i.e. Council Regulation (EEC) No. 2658/87 on the tariff and statistical nomenclature and on the common customs tariffs].

House building cost index: The house building cost index is based on a typical house built in 1975 in the framework of the State housing policy. The index covers only local authority housing.

Wholesale prices index of materials: Covers a selected list of building materials, and excludes water and sanitary services.

Geographic area covered

The house building cost index relates to the area of Dublin: Capital City.

Items included

House building cost index: Measures the change in the cost of building a standard house in 1975 in terms of materials and labour costs. These costs normally do not exceed 65 per cent of the total price of the house.

Wholesale prices index of materials: Show the evolution of wholesale prices (VAT excluded) as reported by enterprises using the materials. Home produced and imported materials are covered.

Capital goods price index: Aims to estimate the cost of construction taking into account labour costs and prices of materials. It is obtained by combining the price of materials index with hourly wage rates obtained from the quarterly average earnings and hours worked survey.

Sources of data

The data used for the three indices come from distinct statistical surveys based on stratified samples.

Method of compilation

House building cost index: Relates to costs (construction materials and labour) ruling on the first day of each month.

The monthly price ratio for each of the commodity headings are generally derived as a simple arithmetic average of the monthly ratio for the constituent items surveyed. These commodity price ratios are combined to produce the published price indices.

Compilation of weights

Wholesale prices index of materials: Uses weights based on the costs of materials used by enterprises as reported in the 1982 Census of Building and Construction.

The weights are taken from national accounts.

Type of index, base year and frequency of compilation

House building cost index: The final index is compiled using the Laspeyres formula.

Wholesale prices index of materials: Is also a Laspeyres index.

Capital goods price index: Is derived from the Laspeyres type wholesale price indices of materials and an hourly wage rate index. The index is rebated every 7 to 8 years.

Data are collected monthly for all three indices.

Use(s) of the index

The capital goods price index is mainly used as deflator for transportable capital.

Publications

Short term production data are released in *Wholesale Price Index*, and *Housing Statistics Bulletin*.

Resume

The Italian Statistical Institute (ISTAT) calculates several input construction indices for the costs of constructing a:

- residential building;
- building for industrial use; and
- for stretches of road.

The indices refer to the base year 1990=100.

The indices are compiled using the standard factors method on the basis of weights representing the proportion of each factor cost to the total cost of the work undertaken in the base period.

Costs index for a residential building: ISTAT has calculated the monthly index for the prices of factors involved in the construction of a residential building, both at provincial and at national levels, since January 1967. The purpose of the index is to monitor the progress over time of the costs that apply to the provision of housing on Italian territory.

Cost index for a building for industrial use: ISTAT has calculated a quarterly index for the prices of factors involved in the construction of a building for industrial use since 1980. The index monitors prices that are meaningful for this type of building. They do not relate to the whole non-residential building construction sector.

Cost index for stretches of road: ISTAT has calculated a quarterly index for the prices of factors involved in the construction of two types of stretches of road (with and without tunnel) since 1980. Road building represents the greatest financial outlay of all civil engineering works undertaken in Italy.

Organisation responsible for index

Istituto Nazionale di Statistica (ISTAT)
Via Tuscolana, 1788
I - 00173 ROMA

Telephone and fax numbers

Tel: (+39) 6 54 900323

Fax: (+39) 6 722 2457

Reference population

Factor prices for a residential building: From the variety of residential buildings constructed, ISTAT has chosen a "standard" building whose characteristics are described in great detail relating to standard categories of works, and exact measurements of the size and volume of the different elements of the building. The cost changes reflected in the index are valid for both the standard building and other buildings which have similar characteristics.

The building consists of three blocks connected by a single service staircase.

Factor prices for a building for industrial use: The standard building for industrial use, which is assumed to be constructed in a provincial capital for each region, is described with the same detail as the residential building, specifying the different types of construction works according to their dimensions.

Factor prices for stretches of road: Index is calculated for two 100 metre stretches of mixed road type - with and without tunnel, using the following roadway typology:

- open air sections (without tunnel)

  - on embankment;
  - in cutting;
  - on viaduct.

- section of road with tunnel

  - open air section,
  - section in a tunnel.

This roadway typology is crossed classified with the five following types of construction work categories:

- movement of materials,
- civil engineering works,
- underground jobs,
- miscellaneous jobs,
- superstructures.

Types of construction covered

Three series of indices are calculated for the factor costs implied by the standard categories of works involved in the construction of a residential building; a building for industrial use; and two types of stretches of road.

The indices are broken down into group indices for labour, materials, and transport and hire.

Each group is further broken down into categories such as skilled workers (in the Labour group), inert materials, binders, or heating equipment (in the Materials group), etc.

Each category includes a number of products for which elementary indices are calculated. For instance, the "inert materials" category includes the following products: sand, gravel, crushed stones.

A different breakdown is used for each index.

Geographic area covered

All indices are calculated on the basis of weights referring to twenty provincial capitals, one per region, excluding the Valle d'Aosta, and including the autonomous province of Bolzano.

The indices for the factor prices of a residential building are calculated not only at the national level, but also for the twenty provincial capitals.

All indices are also calculated for Italy as a whole.

Items included

All three indices measure variations in the direct costs in the construction of a residential building, a building for industrial use, or stretches of road. They do not include the costs of land, planning, job management and connections to the various services. The contractor's profits and margins are also excluded.

The factors for which the prices are monitored are labour, materials, transport, and the hire of machinery.

Sources of data

Factor prices for a residential building: The technical characteristics and the dimensions of the building whose construction costs are monitored have been supplied by the National Association of Construction Contractors (Associazione Nazionale Costruttori Edili - ANCE).

The availability of blueprints and elevations of the building, and detailed metric calculations, combined with the relevant prices, has made it possible to know the overall cost of the construction of the building in each provincial capital considered.

Factor prices for a building for industrial use: The technical characteristics and the dimensions of the building for industrial use whose construction costs are monitored have been supplied by the Ministry of Industry, Commerce and Crafts, in conjunction with the ANCE.

Factor prices for stretches of road: The technical characteristics of the two stretches of mixed road were determined in conjunction with the Autonomous National Road Construction Enterprise (Azienda Nazionale Autonoma delle Strade - ANAS).

Method of compilation

All three indices are compiled using the standard factors method.

The costs for the three types of indices are assessed separately for each of the following three components:

Labour costs: Hourly labour costs are recorded in the same way for the three types of indices. They are different for each category of worker (specialised, skilled, labourer). They are made up of the contractual minimum initial payments, all additional allowances, and the social charges taken from the national contract for workers in the industry, complemented by any provincial contracts. They are recorded by ISTAT.

Prices of materials: Are recorded differently according to the type of index. For the cost of a residential building, and a building for industrial use, the factor prices collected refer to average monthly prices for goods delivered "free to site", excluding VAT. They are recorded by the Statistics Offices at the Chambers of Commerce, Industry, Crafts and Agriculture. Those for Trento and Bolzano are recorded at the Provincial Offices.

For residential buildings, the factor prices incorporate the installation costs excluding the building works.

For the stretches of road, the prices of the materials, excluding VAT, are obtained from the suppliers (quarries, brickworks, manufacturers, wholesalers) for large quantities, and include vehicle loading, packaging and wastage costs, etc. These are collected by the Regional Civil Engineering Offices.

Transport and hire costs: Transport costs refer to quintals per kilometre (q/km) at average distance for the excavation and filler materials.

Hourly hire costs are only considered for machines that have a significant weighting (excavators, diggers, concrete-mixers and cranes).

Transport and hire costs are considered on the basis of actual operating time. They include fuel and/or electricity consumption, and the services of the operator. They are recorded by the Regional Civil Engineering Offices.

Compilation of weights

Factor prices for a residential building: The indices are compiled on the basis of elementary provincial indices. These monitor the price changes of each product in each region. (The breakdown of the indices into groups, categories and products is described above under types of construction covered).

On this basis, indices are compiled for individual categories and groups, aggregate group, as well as at the provincial and national levels. Weights are available for each of these aggregation steps.

Provincial category indices are calculated on the basis of provincial elementary indices corresponding only to the products most commonly used in a given province. In addition, the regional weights for a given product differ from province to province because of the relative differences in prices for the same physical quantity.

Provincial group indices are also calculated.

The national category indices are obtained by aggregating the provincial category indices.

The national group indices are obtained by aggregating the provincial group indices.

The weight of each province used in the calculation of the general index is represented by the value of housing investments made in the region in the period 1988-1990.

The values of the regional investments are divided into each cost category found in the province. These values are converted into provincial weighting coefficients for the calculation of the category index at the national level.

The distribution of the regional investment values in the individual cost group of the respective provinces allows weighting coefficients to be calculated for the provinces in order to determine the indices of each group at national level.

Finally, the weightings of the national group indices for the determination of the general index are respectively: for labour 46.00 per cent; for materials 45.25 per cent; and for transport and hire 8.75 per cent.

Factor prices for a building for industrial use: Weights are represented by the regional investment values, which are translated into national weighting values in the following way:

The values of the regional investments in the period 1988-90 in non-residential buildings for industry were attributed to the province belonging to the region, and distributed among the individual products on the basis of the proportion of the product in total construction in the province. The sum of the provincial values of each product gives the weight of the item for the aggregation of the national indices.

Factor prices for stretches of road: Weights used to aggregate the elementary indices into group indices and into national indices, are obtained from the ratio between the partial costs and the total costs of the work carried out in the base year, broken down according to the roadway typology and type of work categories (refer "Reference population" above).

Type of index, base year and frequency of compilation

The construction costs indices for a residential building are compiled monthly.

The construction costs indices for a building for industrial use, and for stretches of road are compiled quarterly.

Factor prices for a residential building: The elementary provincial indices are obtained by relating the cost observed during the month in question to the average monthly cost recorded in the base year 1990.

The provincial indices of category and group, and the general province index, are obtained by aggregating the respective provincial elementary indices using the Laspeyres formula.

The national category and group indices are obtained by aggregating the provincial indices. However, the national general index is obtained from the national group indices.

Factor prices for building for industrial use: Are compiled according to the Laspeyres formula. The elementary provincial indices, referring to each cost item in each provincial capital, are calculated. The cost recorded in one quarter is related to the average costs of 1990.

The provincial indices are weighted together to obtain the national elementary indices. The national categories and group indices, and the general national index, are then obtained using weighted arithmetic averages.

Factor prices for stretches of road: Various specific indices are compiled according to the roadway typologies (listed above) and the type of work categories. Each index is broken down into elementary indices according to factor types. The weightings attributed to each factor differ with respect to the roadway typology and the type of work categories.

The national indices are compiled according to the Laspeyres formula.

The base year for the three series of indices is 1990=100.

Publications

All indices are published at group and category levels, but not at the product level.

The indices for stretches of road are published according to the roadway typology, type of work categories, and for the two types of stretches of road (with, and without tunnel) (refer Reference population above).

The indices for the factor prices for the construction of a residential building are published for twenty provincial capitals, one per region, excluding the Valle d'Aosta, and including the autonomous province of Bolzano.

The indices are published in the *Monthly Statistical Bulletin.*

Further details concerning the methodology can be found in the ISTAT publication *Numeri indici del costo di costruzione - base 1990=100, Metodi e Norme - edizione 1994* (Construction costs index numbers - base 1990=100, Methods and Standards - series A - No. 29, 1994 edition).

Resume

The construction price index calculated in the Japanese Ministry of Construction is based on input costs.

Organisation responsible for index

Statistics Bureau
Statistical Standards Department
Management and Co-ordination Agency
19-1 Wakamatsu-cho
Shinjuku-ku
Tokyo 162

Telephone and fax numbers

Tel: (+81 3) 5273 1145

Fax: (+81 3) 5273 1181

Types of construction covered

The indices cover most of the construction field, new construction of residential and non-residential buildings, and private civil engineering works.

Items included in the indices

Elements included in the indices are: the costs of materials and labour, and installation costs for water, gas, electricity, bathroom, kitchen, and outside fittings.

The prices used in calculation of the index include tax elements. They reflect discounts.

Sources of data

The price data are obtained from a variety of sources. These include price lists of building materials and service enterprises published by the Bank of Japan, input weights from the producer price tables in input-output tables.

The labour costs data are based on rates set in collective wage agreements and are obtained from surveys of employers. They include social contributions paid by employers.

Method of compilation

About 200 individual input items are costed for the index, these being combined into 26 groups.

Input weights of construction materials, labour, etc. allowing precise calculation of weights are available from input-output tables only every five years . The aggregation of individual indices are based on estimates of investments in construction.

Type of index, base year and frequency of compilation

The index is calculated monthly at the aggregate level using the Paasche formula, given that weights at the main aggregate level are obtained annually. The indices for the individual items that make up the index are calculated as a Fisher Approximate Value, derived by combining the Laspeyres index with an approximate Paasche index using current weights estimated by adjusting base period weights in line with price changes.

The index has the fiscal year 1985 as reference base.

Use(s) of index

The construction price index is intended for use as a construction cost deflator.

Publications

The index results are published in *Monthly Construction Statistics* and various other publications. Results are given for construction as a whole and by type of construction.

Resume

The Bank of Mexico calculates a monthly price index for construction using the standard factors method.

Organisation responsible for index

Banco de Mexico
Gerencia de Informacion Economica
Av. Juarez No. 90
8 Piso, Col. Centro
Mexico, D.F., C.P. 06059

Telephone and fax numbers

Tel: (+52) 521 9047

Fax: (+52) 512 4813

Types of construction covered

The index measures the monthly change in the cost of 42 construction materials and the cost of 17 labour activities in social housing. Social housing is defined as a dwelling for one or several people with basic services: a bathroom, kitchen, living-room, dining-room, laundry, one or several bedrooms, and for which credits at special rates are granted to persons with fixed revenues for its acquisition.

Geographic area covered

All of Mexico. Cities with less than 60 000 inhabitants according to the 1970 population census are excluded.

Prices are collected in 23 cities throughout the country.

Items included in the indices

The elements included in the index are the cost of materials, including their transport to the site, labour, water, gas and electricity installations costs and bathroom and kitchen fittings.

The prices of the materials used in calculation of the index include VAT, and are net of discounts. Labour costs include social contributions paid by employers.

Sources of data

Prices are collected from enterprises that sell construction materials, from construction companies, and other small companies specialising in construction activities. 2 773 price quotations are made, from 280 enterprises, for the cost of 42 construction materials, and the cost of 17 types of building work.

Labour cost data are based on both minimum wages and surveys of employers.

Method of compilation

All prices are obtained directly by data collectors and are notified on a price quotation register (*registro de cotizaciones*). Prices are collected for construction activities (corresponding to material and labour costs) such as masonry, iron works, carpentry, sanitary hydraulic fittings, electrical fittings, plaster work, painting and floor work.

In each city 59 generic indices (corresponding to the different types of costs) are derived from simple arithmetic monthly averages of price quotations.

Compilation of weights

The index is based on a typical apartment block construction project for which 59 input factors were identified. These are weighted according to their relative importance to the total cost of the project in 1974.

Type of index, base year and frequency of compilation

The index is calculated monthly using the Laspeyres formula with reference base 1974=100.

Publications

Indices other than the all-items national index are calculated for each of the 59 items

The results are published monthly in *Carpeta de Indicadores Economicos,* and *Revista Indices de Precios,* both from the Bank of Mexico.

Examples of some of the 59 items for which index results are published are sand, cement, gypsum, toilet, paint, glass, etc.

Indices for total cost of both construction material and labour are calculated at the national and city levels.

Resume

Three construction price indices are calculated in New Zealand: input price indices covering intermediate consumption (i.e. current purchases excluding labour and capital expenditure); output price indices for the construction industry group measuring changes in the prices of what is produced by businesses predominantly engaged in construction activities; and a capital goods price index which measures price movements in productive capital assets purchased by New Zealand industries.

The methodology for the input price indices for the construction industry group is described below. The output price indices for the construction industry group, and the capital goods price index are described in this publication under Output Price Indices.

Organisation responsible for index

Statistics New Zealand
PO Box 2922
Wellington

Telephone and fax numbers

Tel: (+644) 495 4600

Fax: (+644) 495 4617

Types of construction covered

The input price index for the construction industry group measures movements in the prices paid for their intermediate consumption by businesses predominantly engaged in construction activities. All activities of the construction group are covered in these indices, including non-characteristic activities.

Items included in the indices

The input price index for the construction industry group paid for by the industry covers intermediate consumption, i.e. current purchases of the industry, but not capital expenditure or labour inputs. The main elements normally included are: materials (including the cost of transport to the site), equipment hire, land preparation costs (but not land purchase costs), permits, bathroom, kitchen and outside fittings, overheads, and indirect trade margins (i.e. on materials, etc.). Direct margins are excluded.

Professional fees are included to the extent that they are paid by the construction industry firm . However, the building owners often hire their own architect, engineer, etc. in which case these costs do not enter into the index.

Sources of data

The data used in the indices are obtained from a variety of sources. Construction and other enterprises are a major direct source, while some data collected in the first instance for use elsewhere in the producers price index are also used for the construction price index. Use is also made of the publication, *New Zealand Building Economist*, which gives regional estimated prices for installed work.

Method of compilation

A number of models and projects are used in the compilation of the indices. Two approaches are taken.

A range of 18 models, derived from schedules of quantities, is priced each quarter. These models span a wide field, from school and office buildings to factories, sheds, and a church. Prices for installed work are used together with some material, labour and plant prices.

More generalised models are used for a range of disparate project types, ranging from road and railway construction, through to water and gas supply, to car park and power line construction, and irrigation schemes. For these, most pricing is carried out at the work phase level, e.g. earthworks, metalling, sealing, or at the materials/labour/plant level.

The list of models and projects used is reviewed at approximately ten-yearly intervals. The projects themselves have mostly not been revised since the early 1980s.

Compilation of weights

The price indices for the various projects that are priced are combined using weights based primarily on the 1984/85 Census of Building and Construction.

Type of index, base year and frequency of compilation

The Laspeyres formula is used to calculate the index.

The indices are calculated quarterly using the fourth quarter of 1989 as a base. For publication, however, the indices are spliced to the standard Producers Price Index based on the fourth quarter of 1982 (taken as equal to 1 000).

Publications

The index results are published in a variety of outlets including the monthly bulletin *Key Statistics*, the quarterly information release *Hot Off The Press*, and through the on-line system INFOS.

Resume

Statistics Norway has calculated monthly construction cost indices for residential buildings since 1978. Quarterly construction cost indices for civil engineering works have been calculated since 1985.

The indices are compiled using the standard factors method on the basis of weights obtained from cost studies of a sample of completed buildings.

These indices are used to regulate costs of construction works.

Statistics Norway also compiles a quarterly output construction price index for detached houses. This is described in this publication under Output Price Indices.

Organisation responsible for index

Statistics Norway
Division for Construction and Service Statistics
P.O.B. 1260
N-2201 Kongsvinger

Telephone and fax numbers

Tel: (+47) 62 88 54 27

Fax: (+47) 62 88 54 62

Reference population

Prices are collected for a representative basket of materials based on studies of construction projects. The price information is obtained from a sample of suppliers to the construction industry.

The price of labour is evaluated through analysis of annual changes in collective agreements and in social costs. Wage increases in excess of the collective agreement are not included, neither is the VAT.

Types of construction covered

The construction cost indices are broken down by a classification by types of works appropriate to each type of construction.

For every type of work a total cost index and a material cost index are calculated and published. Aggregated indices for the total residential buildings, or civil engineering works are not calculated.

Construction cost indices for residential buildings: Cover input factors used in the construction of three categories of residential buildings: detached houses, row houses, and multi-dwelling buildings.

Construction cost indices for civil engineering works: Cover road construction, maintenance of roads, and water power plants.

Items included in the indices

The construction cost indices show the evolution of the costs of construction of three categories of new residential buildings, and three categories of civil engineering works.

The prices are measured as a weighted average of three input factors: labour, materials and machinery. The factor price index does not include productivity, margins and taxes linked to construction activity. Architects and administrative fees, price of land, connection to road, water and sewerage services and other costs, are also excluded.

Method of compilation

Both series of indices are calculated using the standard factors method.

Residential buildings: Data are collected through monthly surveys of 180 price materials. About 320 suppliers to the construction industry (mainly wholesale companies) provide prices as at the 15th of each month. In addition, some prices are obtained from existing price statistics calculated by Statistics Norway.

Civil engineering works: The necessary input data are mainly obtained from existing indices published by Statistics Norway.

Compilation of weights

Residential buildings: Weights are based on cost studies of a sample of completed buildings. The building work is divided into twelve construction work categories. Each component a structure is defined in terms of percentage of input factors (labour, material and machinery) necessary to carry out this particular work.

The basket of materials for each category is broken down to a representative list of materials for which the weights are also predefined.

The weights for residential buildings were updated in 1990.

Civil engineering works: Weights for the two road indices are based on specifications from the national road authority. The weights for roads were updated in 1991.

The weights for power plants are based on a power plant project completed in 1980.

Type of index, base year and frequency of compilation

The indices are calculated according to a Laspeyres formula.

The base years used for the various indices are as follows:

- Detached wooden houses: 1978=100;
- Terraced wooden houses: 1978=100;
- Multi-dwellings houses: 1978=100;
- Main road and provincial road: First quarter 1985=100;
- Maintenance of main road and provincial road: First quarter 1985=100;
- Water power plant: First quarter 1985=100.

The construction cost indices for residential buildings are compiled monthly. The construction costs indices for civil engineering are compiled quarterly.

Use(s) of the index

These indices are used to regulate the cost of construction works.

Publications

Detailed breakdowns are published by type of works in the monthly construction statistics review *Bygginfo.*

72

Resume

The Portuguese National Institute of Statistics (INE) calculated an index of civil construction in Lisbon based on a March 1949 reference month until 1987.

To renew the old methodology and to meet national needs, INE created a Construction Cost Index for Residential Buildings for the whole of Portugal (excluding overseas territories) in 1988.

The indices are compiled using the standard factors method taking account of materials and labour.

Organisation responsible for index

Instituto Nacional de Estatistica
Gabinete de Estudos Económicos
Avenida Antonio José de Almeida, 5
P-1078 LISBOA

Telephone and fax numbers

Tel: (+351) 1 847 00 50

Fax: (+351) 1 848 10 30

Other organisation involved

The index produced by INE is only a small part of a larger system of price indices developed under the responsibility of the Commission of Indices and Contract Escalation Formulae (CIFE).

Types of construction covered

The index includes labour and materials used in the construction of residential buildings. It covers all buildings under construction.

Geographic area covered

The price indices used in the composition of the index cover the whole of Portugal (excluding overseas territories).

Items included in the indices

The standard factors included in the indices are construction materials and labour.

The prices of materials are based on producer price indices for eight families of products (steel bars, bituminous, cement, red ceramics, blue ceramics, floor tiling, special and exotic woods, and uncoated copper wire).

The labour costs refer to the costs borne by construction enterprises in the Lisbon Capital City area.

Sources of data

The basic information used for the prices of materials corresponds to producer price indices compiled by INE.

The labour costs indices are provided by the Ministry of Qualification and Employment.

Method of compilation

The indices are compiled using the standard factors method.

In 1988, the indices were first calculated on the basis of the value reached by the old index in the last period covered, and on price indices compiled by the CIFE, the Council of Private and Public Construction Works (CMOPP), and the Ministry of Social Equipment.

Since then, in each period, a change rate is applied to the theoretical value of the new index in the previous period.

The indices compiled by the CIFE are used for the revision of prices of contracts signed between the State and private persons, and between private persons.

For this purpose, the CIFE calculates:

Every month, the estimated values of 57 indices showing the evolution of the producer prices of several families of materials (16 with reference period March 1968, and 41 with reference period December 1991). These indices are representative at the continental territory level.

Every quarter, the estimated values of an index representing the evolution of the labour costs borne by construction enterprises (with reference period January 1975). These indices represent five occupations broken down into 18 occupation categories.

Compilation of weights

The formulae used to compile the indices are based on fixed weights. The legislation concerning the revision of contract prices provides formulae to calculate several composite indices, according to the type of construction. For each type of construction the legal text provides, as an indication, a weight structure.

The weights structure for roads (compiled only by CIFE), and residential buildings (INE) are for example:

Standard factor	coeff.	roads	resident. building
Salaries (S)	u	0.38	0.50
Steel bars M_0	b_0	0.08	0.07
Steel cope M_1	b_1	0.10	--
Bituminous M_2	b_2	0.08	0.02
Cement M_3	b_3	0.02	0.07
Explosives M_4	b_4	0.06	--
Diesel M_5	b_5	0.15	--
Pine tree M_6	b_6	0.01	0.04
Red Ceramics M_7	b_7	--	0.05
Blue ceramics - earthenware tiles M_8	b_8	--	0.02
Special and exotic woods M_9	b_9	--	0.06
Uncoated copper wire M_{10}	b_{10}	--	0.02
Sandstone pipes M_{11}	b_{11}	--	--
Fibrocement pipes M_{12}	b_{12}	--	--
Constant C	c	0.12	0.15

These detailed weights were first defined in August 1975, together with the definition and coding of the indices. They were last revised in 1990.

Type of index, base year and frequency of compilation

The formulae used to compile the indices have the following form (referring to the weights structure described above):

$$I_t = u \frac{S_t}{S_0} + b_0 \frac{M_{0t}}{M_{00}} + b_i \frac{M_{it}}{M_{i0}} + C$$

The indices are compiled monthly and refer to the base year 1990=100.

Publications

The construction cost index for residential buildings under construction is published by INE. All other indices are published by the CIFE.

Resume

The Ministry of Civil Engineering Works (Ministerio de Fomento - formerly MOPTMA: Ministerio de Obras Públicas, Transportes y Medio Ambiente) calculates input price indices for the construction industry as a whole as well as for the building and civil engineering sectors. These indices follow the evolution of prices of the inputs contributing to construction activity. They are used to deflate the value of construction in order to estimate a volume index of production.

A seller's price index showing the average price per square metre of dwellings is also compiled. This is described in this publication under Seller's Price Indices.

Organisation responsible for index

Ministerio de Fomento
Dirección General de Programación Económica y Presupuestaria
Paseo de la Castellana, 67
E- 28071 Madrid

Telephone and Fax numbers

Tel: (+34) 1 - 597 82 72

Fax: (+34) 1 - 597 85 24

Types of construction covered

Spain uses the national classification of activities CNAE 74 to determine the units to be surveyed. The activities covered are those defined in this classification, however the Ministry plans to use CNAE 93 (in line with NACE Rev.1) in 1997. This will mean all activities concerning construction of buildings, civil engineering works, or the repair, installation and completion of buildings or civil engineering works.

Nevertheless, a classification by type of work is used for the presentation of the results.

Geographical area covered

The geographical area covered is all the national territory classified by the 17 "Comunidades Autónomas".

Items included

The construction cost index shows the evolution of the cost for construction activity incurred by the constructor. It is used to deflate the value of the production in order to obtain a measure of the volume of production. The components of the costs are intermediate consumption, labour costs, and gross operating surplus. The value of land is not included. The components of intermediate consumption are mainly raw materials.

Sources of data

The elements of the construction cost index are obtained from indices already available from other sources: Producer Price Indices calculated by the Spanish Statistical Office (INE) are used to compile the index of intermediate consumption. The labour cost index is calculated from the tables of wages present in collective agreements of each provincia.

Method of compilation

The total construction cost index is calculated by aggregating two indices: the price index of intermediate consumption and the labour cost index.

The structure of intermediate consumption is obtained using weights derived from the 1990 structural enquiry. The resulting weights are:

- Raw materials (cement, iron & steel, ceramic products, tiles, etc.): 78,77%.

- Other expenses: 21,23%; including

- the renting of equipment represents 1/3;

- financial expenses represents 1/4; and the rest are

- transport expenses, etc.

For practical reasons, the price index of intermediate consumption only includes raw materials. This index shows the evolution of the prices of raw materials and is calculated by weighting the Producer Price Indices (source INE) according to weights derived from the 1990 structural enquiry. The consumption of energy (electricity, coal, gas oil, etc.) is also included in this index.

In order to calculate the labour cost index, the total labour costs for each salary component (base salary, holidays, extra payments, transport payments and social contributions) are weighted according to the number of annual working days and for 12 occupation categories (architect, foreman, specialist, worker, etc.), and an index for each provincia is calculated. These indices are weighted by the number of persons employed in each provincia in order to obtain a national index.

Method of weighting

The weights used to calculate the construction cost index are obtained using weights derived from the 1990 structural enquiry. The weights correspond to intermediate consumption and wages and salaries and are available for total construction as well as for building and civil engineering.

These weights are:

	Total construct.	Building	Civil Engnr.
Intermediate Consumption	62.78%	63.26%	61.31%
Labour Costs	37.22%	36.74%	38.69%

The weights of a list of 35 raw materials used to calculate the price index of intermediate consumption are also obtained from the results of the 1990 structure enquiry. These weights are also available for building and civil engineering.

For instance:

	Total construct.	Building	Civil Engnr.
Iron & Steel	12.1%	11.9%	12.8%
Cement, plaster	19.4%	18.4%	23.8%
Ceramic products.	4.4%	5.2%	1.1%
Electrical cables	3.6%	4.1%	1.3%
Electricity	0.38%	0.32%	0.63%
etc.	...	...	...

Type of index, base year and frequency of compilation

The construction cost index is a Laspeyres index. It is calculated from the price index of intermediate consumption and the labour cost index which are also Laspeyres indices. The base year is 1990.

The price index of intermediate consumption is calculated monthly. The labour cost index is calculated quarterly. The total construction cost index is calculated quarterly.

Use(s) of the index

The construction cost indices are used to deflate the value of production series in order to obtain the volume index of production for the total construction industry, and for the building and civil engineering sectors.

Publications

The construction cost index is available for the following activities:

- total construction industry,
- building sector,
- civil engineering sector.

The price index of intermediate consumption is also available for the same activities. It covers the period 1980 to the present.

The construction cost indices are published by the Ministerio de Fomento in *Boletín estadístico*. The publication is also available on floppy disk which includes historic information and software to manipulate the data.

The methodology used to compile the input price indices was published in 1995 in *Boletín estadístico. Notas metodológicas* (ISBN 84-498-0077-3).

Resume

Statistics Sweden has calculated two types of indices to estimate the price development of input costs involved in the building process since 1910:

- The "contractor's costs index" takes account of the costs for the contractor. The index is calculated both with and without architect's fees.

- The "total factor price index" which also includes other client's costs (such as mortgage and interest rates) and architect's fees. This index monitors the input costs from the client's point of view and doesn't take account of changes in productivity and profit margins. This type of index is not common practice in other countries.

These two input price indices are calculated in two versions, one including wage drift, the other excluding wage drift. The index including wage drift is calculated both with and without VAT. Other input price indices are calculated for repair and maintenance in multi-dwelling buildings and for agricultural buildings.

An output price index for residential buildings is also compiled in Sweden. This is described in this publication under Output Price Indices.

Organisation responsible for index

Statistiska Centralbyrån SCB (Statistics Sweden)
Karlavägen, 100
Box 24 300
S - 115 81 STOCKHOLM

Telephone and fax numbers

Tel: (+46) 8 783 46 31

Fax: (+46) 8 783 49 05

Reference population

The prices for materials are obtained from suppliers to construction contractors and investors. Transport costs are reported separately.

The price of labour correspond to wages calculated through changes in current collective agreements, social security contributions and similar costs.

Types of construction covered

Indices are calculated separately for:

- multi-dwellings buildings (excluding wages drift and VAT);

- collectively built one or two-dwelling buildings (excluding wages drift and VAT);

- maintenance costs in multi-dwelling buildings (including VAT);

- agriculture buildings (excluding wages drift and VAT);

- multi-dwelling and collectively built one or two-dwelling buildings (including wages drift incl./excl. VAT).

The input price indices cover input factors used in the construction of new residential buildings, agricultural buildings and in the repair and maintenance of multi-dwellings buildings.

Geographic area covered

The indices are calculated for the whole of Sweden.

Items included in the indices

The input price indices estimate the relative change in the cost elements involved in the building process. The indices do not measure productivity changes. They also do not reflect profit margins.

Indices are available for the following breakdown by cost elements:

1. materials for:
    - building works
    - building services
    - electricity

2. wages and salaries (excl. wages drift)

3. machinery

4. transport

5. Expenses for:
    - civil servant wages
    - other

(1-5) **contractor's costs for:**
    - all building works
    - subcontracted building works
    - building service installation
    - electrical installation

(1-5) contractor's costs index (incl. architect's fees)

6. Other client's costs
    - Architects fees

(1-6) **total factor price index**

Sources of data

Data for the input price indices are obtained through surveys conducted by Statistics Sweden using questionnaires.

The sample is based on a judgmental selection of enterprises and goods.

Method of compilation

The indices calculation is based on representative standard goods for which prices are obtained from price lists.

Compilation of weights

Different items are weighted together to form the input price indices, for example, the materials index.

Different weights are used for the contractor's costs indices and for the client's cost indices. The weights are based on housing cost studies, and statistics from Statistics Sweden.

Type of index, base year and frequency of compilation

The indices are calculated monthly using the Laspeyres formula according to a fixed base.

The weighting system dates back from 1984.

Use(s) of the index

The indices are used for deflation and analyses, and are used as input indices in the consumer price and producer price indices.

Changes in productivity and profits can be estimated by comparing the Swedish building price index and the factor price index.

Publications

All input price indices are released in the publication *Byggindex*.

Resume

The State Institute of Statistics calculates a quarterly building construction cost index based on the standard factor method.

Organisation Responsible for Index

State Institute of Statistics
Prime Ministry
Necatibey Cad. 114
06100 Ankara

Telephone and fax numbers

Tel: (+90) 312 418 50 27

Fax: (+90) 312 417 04 32

Types of construction covered

The purpose of the index is to identify changes in the cost of input items used in construction projects. The index covers the construction of houses and apartments, shops and commercial buildings, medical buildings, schools and cultural buildings, and administrative buildings. In total these categories cover more than 90 per cent of construction activity in Turkey.

Geographic area covered

The index covers all of Turkey.

Items included in the indices

Included in the index are costs of materials, labour and machinery. No taxes are included in the prices used in the calculation of the index, but the prices are net of discounts.

Sources of data

Most of the cost data used are obtained through surveys of construction and other enterprises as well as from price lists. The data are collected from 24 provinces which have been chosen to represent all the regions of Turkey. Price quotations are obtained for each of the items costed from three establishments in each province. In total, 295 items are priced from around 1 300 suppliers to construction firms.

Method of compilation

The selection of items for inclusion in the index was made after extensive consultation with interested bodies, including the Finance and Industry Statistics Divisions within the State Institute of Statistics, the Chamber of Civil Engineers and of Architects, trade unions and a number of other institutions and associations.

With the help of the Turkish Scientific and Technical Resource Institution and their publication *Construction Unit Price Analysis*, the items were selected and weights determined through detailed examination of bills of quantities for a sample of current projects representative in terms of regional distribution and project type of construction activity within the scope of the index.

Type of index, base year and frequency of compilation

The index is calculated quarterly according to the Laspeyres formula.

The index has base period 1991=100.

Publications

The index results are published by the State Institute of Statistics in the publication *Quarterly Building Construction Cost Index*. In addition to the aggregate results, separate indices are published for materials, machinery and labour costs, as well as for apartments, houses, other construction.

The methodology used in the compilation of the index is published in *Methodology of the Building Construction Cost Index*.

Regional results as well as national indices for Turkey are presented.

Resume

The system of construction cost indices in Great Britain includes construction material cost indices and indices of construction industry wages compiled by the Department of Environment (DOE) using data collected by the Office for National Statistics (ONS). Separate indices are compiled for the costs of materials, and for construction industry average earnings.

The indices are compiled using the standard factors method on the basis of weights reflecting the relative value of purchases of these materials, and components for new housebuilding, other new work, repair and maintenance, and for the whole range of construction activity.

Several output price indices are also compiled in Great Britain. These are described in this publication under Output Price Indices.

Organisation responsible for index

Department of Environment (DOE)
Room P1/016
2 Marsham Street
LONDON SW1 P 3EB

Telephone and fax numbers

Tel: (+44) 1 71 276 47 64

Fax: (+44) 1 71 276 38 26

Types of construction covered

Data are presented according to the following classification:

- new housebuilding,
- other new work,
- repair and maintenance,
- whole range of construction activity.

The producer price indices used to compile the material cost index are calculated for a number of categories of material: bricks (facing, engineering, common), concrete building blocks, sand and gravel, crushed rock, cement, fibre cement products, concrete roofing tiles, ready mixed concrete, slate.

The index of average earnings covers total wages and salaries for manual and non-manual employees combined, employed by enterprises in the construction sector (NACE Rev.1 division 45).

Geographic area covered

The geographic area covered is Great Britain. Northern Ireland, the Isle of Man, and the Channel Islands are excluded.

Items included in the indices

Material cost indices: Are produced by combining a wide range of producer price indices for building materials and components, using weights reflecting the relative value of purchases of these materials and components for new housebuilding, other new work, repair and maintenance and for the whole range of construction activity.

Index of average earnings: Covers total wages and salaries for manual and non-manual employees combined. The index reflects changes such as the number of overtime hours worked, short-time, payments by results, numbers of employees, and different occupations, as well as changes in wage rates.

Sources of data

Data are obtained from a survey using questionnaires, and partly from professional associations. The sample is derived by systematic sampling.

Method of compilation

The indices are compiled using the standard factors method (materials and labour).

Compilation of weights

The weights of the material cost indices are rebated to reflect the materials currently being used.

Type of index, base year and frequency of compilation

The indices are calculated monthly according to a Laspeyres formula with base year 1990.

Use(s) of the index

Material and labour costs indices are used as deflators for the repair and maintenance output series (at constant prices).

Publications

All construction cost indices are published quarterly for the whole construction industry, and for the following breakdown:

- New Housing
- Other New Work
- Repair and maintenance
  - Housing
  - Other work

Data are published monthly in the ONS *Monthly Bulletin of Indices* and quarterly in the DOE release *Housing and Construction Statistics*. Indices are also available quarterly on subscription.

C. OUTPUT CONSTRUCTION PRICE INDICES

AUSTRALIA

Resume

The Australian Bureau of Statistics (ABS) compiles three output price indices for: the construction and renovation of houses; construction of other dwellings; and construction of other buildings. These are described below.

The index for the construction and renovation of houses is calculated quarterly.

The indices for the construction of other dwellings, and the construction of other buildings are proxy output indices calculated monthly. Both indices are calculated by the Australian Construction Services (ACS), which is part of the Commonwealth Department of Administrative Services.

The ABS also compiles price indices based on input costs covering civil engineering works. This is described in this publication under Input Price Indices.

Organisation responsible for index

Australian Bureau of Statistics
PO Box 10
Belconnen, ACT 2616

Telephone and fax numbers

Tel: (+616) 252 6808

Fax: (+616) 252 5327

Types of construction covered

The index for the construction and renovation of houses covers privately-built houses. Only "project homes" (dwellings constructed on the basis of a standard design) are included in the index. The index covers both construction of new houses, and alterations and additions

The indices for the construction of other dwellings, and the construction of other buildings, cover privately-built dwellings other than houses (e.g. apartments, etc.), and non-residential buildings.

No composite index is prepared.

Geographic area covered

The three indices are compiled for each of the eight States and Territories in Australia. Only construction activity in each of the eight capital cities is included.

Items included in the indices

Construction and renovation of houses: Cover the cost of labour, materials (including transport to the site), and equipment hire, plus the installation (but not connection) of water, gas, electricity and telephone services. Internal fittings are included, though an attempt is made to exclude everything which is not under the roofline. Architects' fees, trade margins, overheads, profits and the interest costs of building contractors are also included.

Taxes on material inputs are included in the prices, but not duties related to the final sale. The prices are net of any discounts that apply.

Construction of other dwellings; and other buildings: Among the elements included in the indices are: the cost of labour, materials (excluding cost of transportation to the site), equipment hire, and land preparation costs (excluding the costs of land purchase), installation costs of services and fittings, trade margins, overheads and profits. Indirect taxes are included, as are discounts where possible.

Sources of data

Construction and renovation of houses: A representative sample of projects is obtained in each of the eight capital cities, a total of

110 projects. This ranges from 20 in the larger States, to 8 in the smaller States and Territories. The data are obtained from major construction enterprises.

Price information for project homes is obtained at the end of each quarter from a sample of project home builders in each city.

Sale prices of established houses are obtained from real estate organisations and government agencies. They relate to actual sales transacted during the quarter.

Construction of other dwellings; and other buildings: Uses information from a number of sources, including a sub-set of the 150 cost indices maintained by the ACS.

Construction material prices are generally obtained either from ABS publications or by telephoning suppliers and making adjustments for known biases. The latter method is also used for other intermediate inputs. In addition, information is obtained from tenders, and profit mark-ups are obtained from local master builders and their associations.

Data on wage rates are based on the system of pay "awards", which set the legal minimum pay for each classification within an occupation. Adjustments are applied to allow for payment above the minimum rate and for changes to non-wage labour costs. Social contributions paid by employers are not included.

Method of compilation

Construction and renovation of houses: The indices are compiled using the matched model method and is based on a representative sample of privately built project houses whose prices are monitored from one quarter to the other, and the price movements for each model weighted together.

Construction of other dwellings; and other buildings: Are compiled using the component cost method. This entails the specification of a representative building project as a model. For these indices the models comprise a small apartment block, and a composite of various types

of non-residential building for each of the eight capital cities.

The significant items of expenditure for the project are identified. From an examination of a range of building projects about 75 per cent of the total cost is determined by 25 per cent of the major components of a bill of quantities. To minimise the cost of establishing and maintaining cost indices, the value of each of the less significant items is added to that of the cost-significant item most akin to it, that is one which would be expected to have a similar growth rate.

For each significant item a cost index is derived as the weighted average of the wage, material and other imputed costs. The ACS maintains a range of about 150 cost indices. Each represents a trade or a trade sub-section, etc. and is a weighted average of wage rate indices and price indices for intermediate inputs. To each cost index a variable mark-up is applied to take account of overheads, contractors' risk and profit. Only a sub-set of the 150 cost indices are used in the compilation of the ABS cost index.

The total project cost is derived by combining the component cost indices on the basis of information relating to the total project specifications. The ACS determined the cost of each of the components of the buildings using a bill of quantities for a model project for each building type provided by the ABS in the early 1980s.

Compilation of weights

Construction and renovation of houses: The sample of projects is priced on a quarterly basis and is subject to continuous review. The projects themselves are respecified on a cyclical basis with on average a particular project being included in the sample for a period of two to three years. The various sample projects are equi-weighted within each state.

Construction of other dwellings; and other buildings: Quarterly cost estimates are produced for a small apartment block, and for a composite of various types of non-residential building for each of the eight capital cities. These use a bill of quantities for a model project for each building type supplied by the ABS in the early 1980s. The base period costs of each component are extrapolated forward using cost indices developed by the ACS.

Type of index, base year and frequency of compilation

The Laspeyres formula is used for the compilation of the construction and renovation of houses indices. Construction of other dwellings and other buildings indices is essentially a Laspeyres index, though the composition of the significant cost item components does vary over time.

The indices for the construction and renovation of houses currently have base year July 1989 to June 1990=100.

The reference period for both construction of other dwellings, and other buildings indices is July 1989 to June 1990=100.

Data for the construction and renovation of houses are collected quarterly. Data for construction of other dwellings and other buildings are collected monthly.

Use(s) of index

The indices for the construction and renovation of houses are compiled for use in the compilation of the Australian consumer price indices, and for deflation of corresponding aggregates in the Australian national accounts.

The indices are also used to derive quarterly constant price estimates of approvals, commencements, completion, and value of work done for each State and Territory.

Publications

Construction and renovation of houses: The overall index results are not published separately but are consistent with the total implicit price deflator for dwelling construction as published quarterly in *Australian National Accounts: National Income, Expenditure and Product* and the *State Accounts*. The component home price indices are published in *House Price Indices: Eight Capital Cities* (ABS Cat. No. 6416.0). Separate

indices for the construction of new houses and for alterations and additions are available on request.

Construction of other dwellings; and other buildings: The index results are not published separately but are consistent with the aggregate dwelling and non-dwelling building and construction implicit price deflators as published quarterly in *Australian National Accounts: National Income, Expenditure and Product* (ABS Cat. No. 5206.0) and the *State Accounts* (ABS Cat. No. 5242.0). Price indices at a more disaggregate level are available on request.

Indices are calculated for each of the eight States and Territories of Australia.

Resume

The Austrian Central Statistical Office (ÖSTAT) calculates an output price index comprising five broadly similar quarterly sub-indices for:

- construction of residential buildings
- other building construction work
- construction of roads
- bridge building
- other civil engineering work

The indices are compiled using the component cost method.

Organisation responsible for index

Österreichisches Statistisches Zentralamt (ÖSTAT)
Abteilung 3: Produktion und Dienstleistungen
Hintere Zollamtstraße 2b,
A - 1033 WIEN

Telephone and fax numbers

Tel: (+431) 711 28 7065

Fax: (+431) 715 68 29

Reference population

Prices are collected from enterprises involved in construction activity. Enterprises supply prices for consistently-defined types of building operations on the basis of their most recent contract. If there are several contracts available for selection for a reported quarter, the contract selected for price information is roughly equivalent to a four-storey residential building with approximately 20 apartments.

Types of construction covered

Prices are monitored for a number of individual types of building and construction operations meant to be representative for the whole construction process for building and civil engineering. For instance, item 35 in group 8 (roofworks) of the Standard Specification for Building Construction is defined as follows:

> "1 m² of covering roof area with freshly fired clay roofing tiles ...*... cm. Product ...... laid dry, suspended/nailed on prepared battens."

Residential and non-residential buildings: In 1986, the *Standard Specification for Building Construction* [LB-H] recommended for use by the Federal Ministry for Economic Affairs was adopted for the uniform description of twenty individual types of construction operation groups broken down into 82 representative individual types of building operation (see example above).

These 20 types of construction operation are split into building contractor's works (earthworks, bricklayers, etc.) and other building works (joinery, locksmith, electrical installation, etc.).

Residential building price indices: Covers both public and private construction of houses and apartment blocks. Reporting enterprises are asked to supply on a questionnaire, prices from their most recent contracts, some of which should relate to properties equivalent to a four storey block of about 20 apartments, and some to housing estate construction. The index covers land preparation, main building works, installation and completion, and the installation of domestic appliances.

Other building price indices: Encompasses all buildings not intended primarily for residential purposes.

Road construction: For this index, prices are monitored for 19 individual construction operations grouped into the following 5 construction operations groups: earthworks, drainage works, concrete and walling works, paving, surfacing.

Bridge construction: For this index, prices are monitored for 22 individual construction operations grouped into 5 construction operations groups: earthworks and foundation works, concrete and walling works; stone deliveries, sealing works, bridge equipment, surfacing.

Price index for other civil engineering: Other civil engineering in this context covers all civil engineering work that cannot be attributed specifically to road or bridge engineering work. However, it excludes power plants not covered directly in this series of indices.

A survey of activity under the heading other civil engineering revealed that the bulk of the work involved the construction of water supply and sewerage treatment plant. Price observation is therefore restricted to this branch of the activity, which is felt to be representative of the heading other civil engineering as a whole.

For this index, prices are monitored for 23 individual construction operations grouped into the following five construction operations groups: earthworks, pressurised pipelines and drainage sections, mass concrete and reinforced concrete, shaft construction, other building works.

Geographic area covered

The indices are weighted for 9 regions in Austria.

Weights for the road and bridge construction indices also take into account the type of terrain. Each region has percentages of flat, hilly and mountainous terrain.

The total area covered is Austria.

Items included in the indices

For all indices, the prices collected are prices on the basis of concluded contracts. These may not be the final prices, but reflect the prices at the moment of observation. They have the advantage of being available relatively quickly, in contrast to invoice prices.

The indices include the installation costs of water, gas and electricity, and internal fittings.

Excluded are: land purchase and preparation costs, telephone installation costs, external fittings, professional fees.

The prices are net of discounts, and generally do not include VAT.

Sources of data

The price observation method varies by sub-index.

Residential building and other buildings price indices: For residential and other structural building a shuttle questionnaire is sent to the building companies who provide information on a voluntary basis. The approximate number of enterprises reporting prices each quarter for the defined individual work types of buildings is as follows:

- construction of residential buildings   770
- other building construction work   730

Price indices for road construction; bridge construction; and other civil engineering: For roads the provincial construction departments and companies responsible for awarding road building contracts provide the prices to ÖSTAT.

For bridges the provincial construction departments again perform this role.

For other civil engineering, survey questionnaires are sent to provincial construction departments and specialist associations. This approach reflects the public character of these types of construction and reduces the reporting burden on enterprises.

The approximate number of civil engineering projects per quarter reported by provincial construction departments is:

- construction of roads   70
- bridge building   35
- other civil engineering work   80

Method of compilation

The component cost method is based on prices for representative types of construction operations.

For each sub-index a list of types of construction operations is drawn up. Price indices are calculated by forming an average price from the (maximum of eight) price reports received for each individual operation in each Federal State. When compared with the corresponding reference price (average price for the base period), this average price gives an index.

The 738 indices (82 types of construction operations for nine Federal States) produced in this way each quarter are combined to produce Group Indices and the Overall Index for Austria, both through weighting the individual types of construction operations and also by means of regional weighting.

The types of construction operations are identified according to a detailed classification.

Wherever possible the prices are collected for types of construction operations consistently-defined from period-to-period. Where a change in the detailed specification of the work is unavoidable, the change is reported on the questionnaire (with a figure on the new basis also being reported for the previous period) and taken into account by making base adjustments when calculating the current index values.

Residential building price indices: A similar number of prices is collected in each region for each type of construction operations (generally around 5-10 for each individual type of operation for each sub-index) and an average price is calculated for the region. These regional averages are then weighted together using the share of the region in the value of production in the base period.

Other building price indices: Employs a similar methodology to that used for apartment block and housing estate construction. Special care is taken to ensure that the diversity of types of construction operations included are appropriately weighted in the calculation of the final sub-index.

Price indices for road construction; bridge construction; and other civil engineering: For these indices, the weights take into account the nature of the terrain (flat, hilly, mountainous) as well as the region. The same number of projects are drawn randomly for each type of terrain. From these are determined the shares of the work category groups in each project, as well as the share of the work categories within these groups. Thus for each terrain type, the average share of each category group, and category is determined.

These results are weighted using the share of each terrain type in each province to give average weightings of categories and category groups for Austria. These regional weights are based on the shares of the value of road production in the base year.

Compilation of weights

The number of projects used in determining the weights for each sub-index at the last weight review was:

- construction of residential buildings   92
- other building construction work   135
- construction of roads   200
- bridge building   114
- other civil engineering work   141

The group weights and regional weights are not revised at each base change, nor at the same time for each sub-index.

The lists of types construction operations and associated weights are reviewed approximately every ten years.

Type of index, base year and frequency of compilation

All indices are compiled according to the Laspeyres formula.

The reference base year for the overall index is currently 1994, which is always the base year of the most recently revised sub-index.

Sub-indices with other base years are, for the calculation of the overall index, mathematically rebated to this year.

The Austrian index of construction prices, and all sub-indices are compiled quarterly.

Use(s) of the index

The index is used for deflation of national accounts and will also probably be used for the planned production index in construction.

Publications

The residential building sub-index index is also available, broken down between building contractor's work and other building work.

The two sub-indices, residential building and other building construction work are combined to give an index for structural building.

The road construction sub-index is combined with the similarly-constructed sub-index for bridge building to give an index for combined road and bridge building.

The other civil engineering sub-index is combined with those for road and bridge building to give an index for civil engineering as a whole, with a small element being included for power station construction.

The indices for structural building and civil engineering are weighted together to give an overall construction index, using the shares of building output in 1986 as weights.

Finally, the indices are published according to the following breakdown (between brackets, the weight of each sub-index in the overall Building Price Index in 1986).

- **Building price index (BPI)**   **[100%]**

- BPI for Buildings   [55.3%]
  - BPI for residential buildings
    (incl. alterations)   [25.7%]
  - Building Contractor's work
  - Other Building work
  - BPI for Other buildings
    (incl. agricultural)   [29.6%]

- BPI for Civil Engineering   [44.7%]
  - Road construction   [18.0%]
  - Bridge construction   [02.4%]
  - Other Civil Engineering   [24.3%]

The indices are calculated and published only at the national level. No regional breakdown is disseminated.

All the sub-indices and the overall index are published quarterly by ÖSTAT in

- *Statistische Nachrichten*,

- *Schnellbericht - Baupreisindex*

- ÖSTAT database *ISIS*.

Further details on the methodology of the indices are published in *Der Österreichische Baupreisindex 1971-1985, Heft 810, ÖSTAT, Wien 1989* (The Austrian Construction Price Index 1971-1985) and in the following issues of *Statistische Nachrichten:*

- S. N., 46, Jahrgang 1991 (Neue Folge), Heft 6.

- S. N., 43, Jahrgang 1988 (Neue Folge), Heft 6.

- S. N., 40, Jahrgang 1985 (Neue Folge), Heft 11.

Resume

Seven construction price indices are calculated in Canada. These comprise two output, four input, and one seller's price indices. The two output indices described below cover:

- apartment building construction
- non-residential building construction

The seller's price index, and the four input price are described in this publication under Input Price Indices and Seller's Price Indices.

No aggregate index combining the seven separate construction price indices is compiled.

Organisation responsible for Index

Statistics Canada
Jean Talon Building
Tunney's Pasture
Ottawa, Ontario
Canada KIA OT6

Telephone and fax numbers

Tel: (+613) 951 9615

Fax: (+613) 951 2848

Types of construction covered

Apartment building construction: Measure contractors' selling price change of public and private sector apartment building construction.

Non-residential building construction: Measures contractors' selling price change of non-residential construction (i.e. commercial, industrial, and institutional). This quarterly index, which is termed the Canada Composite, is mainly based on the pricing of five standard constructions, representing the three broad categories of construction (commercial, industrial, and institutional), although there is also an input costs element. A sixth model representing hospital construction (in the institutional construction category) will be included in the next addition to coverage by building types.

Geographic area covered

Apartment building construction: The data collected for this index covers about 60 per cent of construction output of apartment blocks. It is restricted to seven cities in five provinces.

Non-residential building construction: The data collected for this index covers about 40 per cent of construction output of non-residential buildings, and is also restricted to seven cities in five provinces.

Items included in the indices

Apartment building construction: The costs covered in the index include most of the main construction items plus kitchen cupboards and carpets, but exclude appliances. The costs of land purchase and preparation, and architects' and engineers' fees, are also excluded. Prices include overheads and profits. Goods and service tax is not included, but other (provincial) taxes are. Prices are net of discounts.

Non-residential building construction: The prices covered in this index are roughly equivalent to those included in the index for apartment building construction. Thus, they include most of the main construction items. The costs of land purchase and preparation, and architects' and engineers' fees, are excluded. Goods and service tax is not included, but other (provincial) taxes are. Prices are net of discounts.

Sources of data

Data for both indices are obtained by a combination of personal visit and telephone from construction and other enterprises, and from producer price index sources. In some cases data on union wage rates are obtained from surveys of employers and signed collective agreements. The labour costs data include selected social contributions paid by employers.

Method of compilation

Both indices are based on the pricing of a standard construction, although there is also an input costs element. The standard construction for the apartment index, which was actually built in Canada in 1981, is a 53 unit reinforced concrete structure with 7 storeys, a basement parking facility and a penthouse unit.

The apartment building construction index standard construction is taken as being representative of both public and private sector apartment building.

The standard constructions for the non-residential building construction index were also actually built in Canada and comprise an office building, a warehouse, a shopping centre, a light industry factory building and a secondary school.

Prices for both indices are obtained from contractors and sub-contractors who construct apartment and/or non-residential buildings, on the basis that they are bidding on a fixed specification and quantity under current market conditions.

It is intended to review the standard projects for both indices at approximately 10-yearly intervals.

Compilation of weights

Apartment building construction: Weights were derived from a detailed cost analysis of the model apartment building. While the standard project is held constant the weights used in combining the various city indices that make up the Canada total are updated annually, in January, in the light of results taken from 36 months of building permit data in relation to the census metropolitan areas (cities). This survey covers about 60 per cent of construction output of apartment blocks, but is restricted to seven cities in five provinces.

Non-residential building construction: Weights are derived from detailed cost analyses of each structure wherein quantities or values for each model were expressed in 1986 price levels. While the standard constructions are held constant the weights used in combining the various building projects and city indices that make up the Canada Composite are updated annually, in January, in the light of results taken from 36 months of building

permit data in relation to the census metropolitan area. This survey covers about 40 per cent of construction output of such projects, but is restricted to seven cities in five provinces.

Type of index, base year and frequency of compilation

Apartment building construction: A fixed weight formula is used at the city level. A chain Laspeyres index formula is used for the seven city composite levels, for which the weights are derived from building permit data for the previous three years, valued at the price levels of the fourth quarter of the last year.

Non-residential building construction: A fixed weighted formula is used at the model level. A chain Laspeyres index formula is used for aggregations at the city and seven city composite levels, for which the weights are derived from building permit data for the previous three years valued at price levels of the fourth quarter of the last year.

Both indices are compiled quarterly and have base year 1986=100 (shortly to change to 1992).

Use(s) of index

These indices are used for a variety of purposes, e.g. deflation of construction industry output, deflation of expenditures on gross fixed capital formation, contract escalation, and asset revaluation.

Publications

Both indices are first published in Statistics Canada, *The Daily* (Cat. No. 11-001E). They are also published quarterly in *Construction Price Statistics* (Cat. No. 62-007). As well as the overall index, indices are also available for individual trade groups (architectural, structural, mechanical, electrical). For the non-residential building construction index indices are available for broad categories of construction (commercial, industrial, institutional).

For both indices data are available for seven cities in Canada.

91

Resume

The Indice du Coût de la Construction (ICC) is a quarterly output price index of new residential buildings calculated and published by INSEE on the basis of data provided by the Ministry of Equipment and Housing.

This index was first created in 1953 to serve as a benchmark for interest rate evolution for a specific type of saving account for potential house buyers.

The ICC is compiled on the basis of a schedule of prices referred to below as the "Bordereau Général d'évaluation des travaux neufs" (BGE).

The current methodology for the ICC is described below. However, the Ministry of Equipment, in collaboration with INSEE, plan to modify this index which method is very costly.

The Ministry of Equipment and the Ministry of Economy also calculate two input price indices described in this publication under Input Price Indices.

The output indices described below are used for deflation of components of the national accounts.

Organisation responsible for index

INSEE
18 Boulevard Adolphe Pinard
F-75675 PARIS - Cedex 14

Ministère de l'Equipement du Transport
 et du Tourisme
Tour Pascal B
F-92055 Paris-La-Défense Cedex 04

Telephone and fax numbers

INSEE

Tel: (+33) 1 41 17 51 15

Fax: (+33) 1 41 17 63 11

Ministère de l'Equipement

Tel : (+33) 1 40 81 28 98

Fax (+33) 1 40 81 28 27

Other organisation involved

Data for the ICC are collected by the sub-directorate for information - Construction statistics, Surveys Office from the Ministry of Equipment.

Reference population

The reference population is defined in terms of houses or buildings with two or more dwellings built during the reference period (one quarter). The statistical information is obtained through building permits linked to these constructions.

The first step is to eliminate those permits that didn't lead to construction and those that do not correspond to residential buildings. For each selected permit, the future owner (maître d'ouvrage) is then contacted and asked to provide the Ministry of Equipment with financial and technical documents related to the construction of the building.

The financial documents (price of works (total or broken down by trade), mode of escalation and revision of prices, reference date for the prices, etc.) are used to calculate the actual and current price of the construction.

The technical documents (plans, description of works, etc.) are used to evaluate with the help of the BGE (see description below) the theoretical price of the construction in the reference year (1987). That is the price that would have been paid for exactly the same building in the base year.

Types of construction covered

The ICC only covers new residential buildings excluding residences for communities (e.g. orphanages, prisons, etc.) and activities linked to repair and maintenance.

For each building selected in the sample, a theoretical base year price is evaluated with the help of the BGE. This is a register containing the unit prices (collected in the base year) for approximately 4 000 elements of construction. These elements are defined according to a functional classification; each element is linked to its main function in the building.

For example, the item external superstructure walls includes the following components: walls, heat insulation, inner coating, openings, balconies, loggia, etc.

In terms of activities, the index does not cover site preparation (NACE Rev.1 group 45.1) and repair and maintenance. The coverage falls partly within NACE Rev.1 groups 45.2, 45.3, and 45.3.

Geographic area covered

The total area covered is metropolitan France (excluding overseas departments and territories).

The database is sorted by region. Five large regions have been defined on the basis of the 22 administrative French regions (excluding overseas départements and territories). These five regions were defined so that each has a similar weight, and differs as much as possible from other regions regarding the construction price level.

Items included in the indices

The ICC shows the evolution of the price paid by the future owner (maître d'ouvrage) of a new building (house or building with two or more dwellings).

Wages for architects or quantity surveyors are not included in the prices collected except in the case of individual houses sold "on catalogue" for which the client pays a global selling price including architects' fees.

Method of compilation

Data for the ICC are collected through building permits and financial and technical files obtained from the client.

The survey is based on a sample. The sample represents the buildings constructed during the reference quarter. The sample for the ICC for month T comprises approximately 1 000 building permits delivered in month $T-2$ randomly selected with probabilities proportional to the size (measured by the number of dwellings in the building). The sample is stratified according to the following criteria:

- type of permit (individual house or multiple dwelling building);
- size;
- sorted by region.

Out of these 1 000 permits those not corresponding to the coverage of the survey are eliminated. Those for which building contracts are not yet signed are kept in a reserve until it is signed. Contracts that were signed more than 9 months before the calculation term are not taken into account.

For each permit selected, the related financial and technical documents are collected from the client.

Approximately 320 to 350 files are normally kept in the final sample. As the sampling rate applied to larger buildings is high, these correspond to around 6 000 dwellings per quarter (6 per cent to 7 per cent of all dwellings built during a quarter).

On the third quarter of the year the procedures for the collection of financial and technical information directly from the client (described above) is very difficult as many people are not available during the summer period. The index for the third quarter of each year is derived from the BT input price indices (refer to Input Price Indices).

A strong and stable relationship can be observed in the past between the ICCs rate of change and that of the BT01. The ICC is then estimated according to the linear relationship between its quarterly growth rate in quarter T and the corresponding growth rates of the BT01 for quarters T and $T-1$.

Compilation of weights

Each construction selected in the sample is weighted according to its size and type:

- individual;
- grouped individual;
- 2 to 9 dwellings;
- 10 to 29 dwellings;
- 30 or more dwellings;
- apartment buildings;
- 2 to 19 dwellings;
- 20 to 49 dwellings;
- 50 or more dwellings.

Type of index, base year and frequency of compilation

The ICC is similar to a Paasche index, the weights are updated every quarter and correspond to the current state of the building trade.

The index corresponds to the ratio of the weighted real average price to the average weighted theoretical price.

The theoretical price (BGE price) calculated on the basis of the technical characteristics of the building is corrected to eliminate the impact of different types of dwelling structures.

The index is expressed in base 100=1953. The base year is the year preceding the reference quarter.

Data for the ICC are collected quarterly except for the third quarter when the index is directly estimated from the input price index BT01.

Use(s) of the index

ICC is used to deflate the value of production for new residential buildings.

Publications

The ICC is published quarterly in *Journal Officiel (JO) de la République Française,* and *Bulletin mensuel de la Statistique (BMS).*

The index is also available on minitel 3615-3616, code INSEE (series starting in 1970).

Finally, the series can be requested by telephone (+33) 1 43 45 70 75.

The methodology of the ICC is further described in *INSEE - Méthodes No.17, février 1992* (INSEE - Methods No.17, February 1992).

Resume

The Federal Statistical Office of Germany (Statistisches Bundesamt) calculates construction price indices for selected important types of construction that fall into two broad groups:

- construction of conventional design, and maintenance of residential building (quarterly)

- single-family houses of prefabricated design (half-yearly)

The first index is compiled using the component cost method and is referred to in this publication as the conventional construction price indices.

The second index was created in 1968 when the construction of prefabricated single-family houses experienced a boom and reached a market share of 10 per cent of total house construction in the mid-1970s. In 1991, system-built houses still represented 7 per cent of the market in the former West Germany. This index is comparable to a producer price index and is referred to in this publication as standard house price indices.

Organisation responsible for index

Statistisches Bundesamt
Gustav-Stresemann-Ring, 11
D 65189 WIESBADEN

Telephone and fax numbers

Tel: (+49) 611 75 2441

Fax: (+49) 611 72 4000

Other organisation involved

Conventional construction price indices: Data collection for these indices is undertaken by the regional Statistical Offices (State Authorities) using methods and instructions provided by the Federal Statistical Office.

Standard house price indices: For these indices, the Federal Statistical Office conducts the price survey, (except in Bavaria where prices are collected by the Bavarian Land Statistical Office).

Reference population

The reporting unit is the enterprise with activities in the building and civil engineering sectors.

Types of construction covered

Conventional construction price indices: The activities covered quarterly by the reference population are almost equivalent to NACE Rev.1 division 45. Reporting units may also be enterprises with secondary activities within division 45. The price indices for structures of conventional design and for the maintenance of residential buildings cover new construction and repairs of a selection of important types of buildings and other constructions.

The indices are based on a selection of representative construction work categories identified according to the "Verdingungsordnung für Bauleistungen" (VOB). This is a classification by type of construction activity.

The VOB is a code for the granting of contracts for the construction of public buildings, but it is often used as the basis of private building contracts as well. Part C of the VOB contains the General Technical Conditions of Contract (ATV), which define all construction work categories (construction services rendered) that are the object of a specific contract between the client and the contractor. In a contract, a price is attached to each of these categories of construction work (tiling, roofing, etc.).

By examining these records, the statistical office defines typical construction work categories as collection items and provides relevant framework descriptions. The reporting firms first add details to the framework description by specifying the way in which they regularly perform the collection item. All further price notifications will refer to these specified construction work categories.

Construction price indices for the individual types of building are shown in a breakdown by types of construction work. Types of construction work are an aggregation of construction work categories, the allocation being made according to the VOB. The breakdown by types of construction work is very detailed, for instance the breakdown for road bridges is as follows:

- earthworks

- roadway construction work, surface layers of asphalt

- concrete and reinforced concrete work

- structural steelworks

- metal work

- scaffolding work

Currently, 220 standard construction work categories are defined as collection items. The relevant prices reported are included in the calculation of construction price indices for nine main types of structure:

- residential buildings;

- non-residential buildings (office / industrial and commercial);

- road construction;

- road bridges;

- sewerage system;

- dams;

- sewerage treatment plants;

- maintenance of residential buildings.

The results are also partially computed for different types of buildings or other constructions. For example, apart from the price index of residential buildings, price indices are computed for single-family houses, multi-family houses, and other residential buildings.

Standard house price indices: Are calculated for the following breakdown:

- system-built houses with system-built or conventionally constructed cellars

- system-built houses without cellars.

The activities cover only the main construction and installation and completion of residential single-family buildings.

Geographic area covered

The territorial classification by 16 Länder is used for the conventional construction price indices for data collection and processing.

The total area covered is Germany after unification, i.e. the borders as of 3 October 1990.

Items included in the indices

For both indices the prices notified are market prices at the time of the award of the contract (not tender prices) excluding VAT. VAT rate changes are reintroduced in the calculation of the index.

Sources of data

All the data used to compile construction price indices are obtained from surveys conducted by the regional and federal statistical offices.

All data collection is done using questionnaires sent and collected by the Regional Offices.

Conventional construction price indices: The reporting unit is the enterprise with activities in the building and civil engineering sectors.

Standard house price indices: The reporting units are chosen from the producers of prefabricated single-family houses. A judgmental sample of reporting units is used.

Method of compilation

Conventional construction price indices: The Regional Offices first calculate for each price notification, the firm's index figure. This is the ratio, multiplied by 100, of the current price of an item of construction work category to the corresponding average price in the base year.

The firm's index figures for a collection item are then averaged and the resulting 220 Land index figures are sent to the Federal Statistical Office.

96

The Federal Office then calculates a federal index figure for each survey heading (construction work categories) by weighting the Land index figures with the construction industry turnovers of the Länder in the base year.

Finally, the federal index figures are weighted by means of structure-specific weighting schemes.

As prices are surveyed excluding VAT, the last stage is to increase (or decrease) the price indices by the change in the tax rate.

Standard house price indices: The price indices for prefabricated design houses are usually producer price indices. The producer can build a number of similar houses for subsequent sale. In this case, the producer price can differ from the purchasing price, and the methods used to calculate the indices are similar to those used for manufacturing industries.

Compilation of weights

Conventional construction price indices: Billing records and invoices are obtained for the building construction categories for given types of structure performed during the base year. Property owners are contacted. For each billing record, the Federal Statistical Office totals the prices of all construction work categories that can be allocated to a specific collection item. This total is then divided by the total price of the structure to obtain the relative weight of the collection item in question.

Because this methodology is very time consuming, weights are only renewed for some of the types of structure. For the 1991 base year, the weights of roads and road bridges were renewed in addition to sewerage treatment plants, which were included for the first time.

The weights for the collection items for the other types of building (and other constructions) are updated according to the price development for the respective types of buildings (and other constructions) since the latest base year.

Standard house price indices: Uses weights corresponding to the proportion of the turnover of the category of reporting firms.

Type of index, base year and frequency of compilation

The indices are calculated according to a Laspeyres formula.

The base year is 1991.

Conventional construction price indices: Data are collected quarterly in February, May, August and November.

Standard house price indices: Data are collected half-yearly. The prices refer to 1 April and 1 October.

Publications

Conventional construction price indices: Is published quarterly for selected types of structures:

- all residential buildings:
  - single-family residential buildings
  - multi-family residential buildings
  - mixed used residential buildings
- office buildings
- all industrial and commercial buildings
  - 2 variants
- total road construction
  - 2 variants
- all road bridges
  - 2 variants
- sewerage system
- dams
- sewage treatment plants
- total maintenance of multi-family buildings
  - 2 variants

Regional indices are available for some Länder, and are published by the respective regional statistical offices. Due to restrictions on confidentiality, and/or smaller databases, regional statistics are more aggregated.

Construction price indices are published in *Meßzahlen für Bauleistungs preise und Preisindizes für Bauwerbe* - (subject matter series 17, series 4) (Index Numbers of Prices for Construction Work

Categories and Price Indices for Buildings and other Constructions).

The methodology is further detailed in *Zur Neuberechnung der Baupreisindizes auf Basis 1991* in *Wirtschaft und Statistik* 1/1191, p.21ff. (New computation of the building price indices with base 1991).

Resume

The National Statistical Service of Greece (NSSG) has calculated a price index of work categories for the construction of new residential buildings since 1980. This index is compiled using the component cost method.

A price index of cost elements covering materials, labour, and other expenditures is also calculated. This is described in this publication under Input Price Indices.

Organisation responsible for index

NSSG - National Statistical Service of Greece
14-16 Lycourgou Street
GR-10166 ATHENS

Telephone and fax numbers

Tel: (+30) 1 32 43 669 / 32 89 509

Fax: (+30) 1 32 23 159

Reference population

The prices are collected from construction enterprises and contractors.

Types of construction covered

The activities related to the construction of new residential buildings are covered by reference to a classification of type of works categories in 19 headings.

Geographic area covered

The indices refer only to buildings constructed in the Greater Athens area which is considered to be representative of all urban areas in Greece.

Items included in the indices

The prices paid for the individual works which comprise the index of work categories of new residential buildings refer to the prices actually paid to subcontractors, and which usually cover expenditures for materials, labour, depreciation of fixed assets, and profit.

Payment agreements for the construction of several sections of the building are made according to type of work categories. Prices refer to the construction work categories, e.g. square or cubic metres, prices of work, etc. according to the kind of work.

Sources of data

Data are collected through statistical surveys conducted by means of telephone enquiries and individual visits.

Reporting units are sampled according to the volume and the value of their transactions.

Method of compilation

The data collected refer to prices agreed during the quarter in review.

Compilation of weights

The weighting coefficients were obtained from an analysis of the accounting records of 150 building enterprises for the period 1988 to 1990.

Type of index, base year and frequency of compilation

The index is calculated quarterly according to a Laspeyres formula.

The base year is currently 1990.

Use(s) of the index

The index is used for statistical purposes such as deflation of national accounts.

Publications

Indices are published in the *Monthly Statistical Bulletin*, the *Statistical Yearbook of Greece*, and in the *Concise Statistical Yearbook*.

Resume

The Statistical Office of Luxembourg (STATEC) has calculated twice yearly price indices for the construction of residential and semi-residential buildings since 1972.

The indices are compiled using the component cost method.

Organisation responsible for index

STATEC
Département des statistiques de court terme
6, Bd. Royal
BP 304
L - 2013 LUXEMBOURG

Telephone and fax numbers

Tel: (+352) 47 84 244

Fax: (+352) 46 42 89

Reference population

Reporting unit: The information is obtained from kind of activity units or enterprises from all trades participating in construction activity.

Observation unit: Prices are collected for standard categories of building covering all types of works involved in the construction of residential or semi-residential buildings.

These categories of building operations are roughly defined by the STATEC. Each reporting unit then amends these definitions according to the details corresponding to the building techniques the enterprise generally use. These specifications allow for clear identification of the building operations priced period after period.

Types of construction covered

The construction price indices cover the construction of new residential and semi-residential buildings. NACE Rev.1 groups 45.1 to 45.4 are partially covered in this respect.

Two types of classifications are used to compile the construction price indices: a classification by type of building, and a nomenclature of standard categories of building operations. The standard buildings are classified as follows:

TYPE A

- Single family detached house
- Built according to individual plans
- Standard built (turnkey house)
- Single family house in rows
- Built according to individual plans
- Standard built (turnkey house)
- Multi-dwelling houses with less than 6 levels

TYPE B

- Multi dwelling houses with 6 or more levels
- Semi-residential buildings
- Mainly residential
- Mainly non-residential

The nomenclature of standard categories of building operations is a 4-digit classification including site preparation, main building works, building installation and building completion.

Geographic area covered

The index relates to the whole area of Luxembourg (country).

Items included in the indices

The indices show the evolution of prices of newly built residential and semi-residential buildings. The price includes all factor prices, as well as margins and productivity changes. The method used to calculate the index is based on the observation of real prices of standard categories of building operations.

Sources of data

Data are obtained through a sample survey of the building sector.

The prices are obtained from the reporting enterprises using questionnaires. During an initial meeting with STATEC agents, the enterprise precisely defines the standard categories of building operations it will report over the next 10 years.

Price changes due to quality changes in the standard operation are eliminated. The price is estimated by the respondent where a category of operation is provided for one or two periods in a form that does not correspond to its definition.

Where the specification of a standard category changes dramatically, the definition is modified accordingly and the new corresponding series are statistically linked to the former one.

When an enterprise in sample disappears it is replaced by another which conducts activities as near as possible to former standard categories of building operations.

The sample comprises 200 enterprises selected according to their main activity and size.

Method of compilation

The index is compiled using the component cost method. A basket of 140 standard categories of building operations is defined and each reporting unit is asked to provide the real price received for each of the standard operations performed in the last six months. Each standard category of building operation is weighted according to its importance in the total cost of a typical building in order to calculate a global index.

Compilation of weights

A basic index is calculated for each standard category of building operation that is weighted according to their respective importance to the total cost of a standard building. These weights are obtained every 10 years from a general survey of architects, building contractors, and real estate developers.

Type of index, base year and frequency of compilation

The indices are compiled according to the Laspeyres formula every 6 months (in April and October).

The base year is currently 1990. It is renewed every 10 years.

Use(s) of the index

The indices are used as an economic indicator, a deflator for national accounts, and as a benchmark for fire insurance contracts, and building and selling contracts in the construction sector.

Publications

The indices are released in the publication *Indicateurs rapides - Série A2*, under the title *Bi-yearly Indices of Construction Prices (Residential and Semi-residential Building*s).

A methodological note on the construction price index was published in *Bulletin du STATEC 1991 No.5* under the title "Méthodologie - Le passage à la base 1990" (Methodology - the change to the base year 1990).

Resume

Statistics Netherlands (the CBS) has calculated the PINB indices, a system of yearly construction price indices for residential buildings of the social rented sector, since 1964.

These indices were compiled using the component cost method based on a detailed analysis of the construction plans collected within the framework of cost-quality evaluation procedures used for public housing policy formulation (e.g. the calculation of subsidies).

The relevant data for these evaluations were collected by the Dutch Ministry of Public Housing, Planning and Environment, and were made available to the CBS.

Responsibility for public housing policy was recently transferred to the municipalities and the required data are now no longer available at the national level. As a result the CBS decided to collect the data for its own needs and to calculate the index using an hedonic price index method. This method is based on a econometric model in which variables correspond to the different price components observed in the costs-quality evaluation procedures involved by the PINB system. The aim of the revised method is to avoid costly and time consuming evaluation procedures.

Both methods are described below.

Organisation responsible for index

Central Bureau voor de Statiestiek/Statistics Netherlands
Prinses Beatrixlaan, 428
Postbus 959
NL-2270 AZ VOORBURG

Telephone and fax numbers

Tel: (+31) 70 337 5522

Fax: (+31) 70 3877 429

Other organisation involved

Data for the PINB were collected by the Dutch Ministry of Public Housing, Planning and Environment. The index was compiled by the CBS.

The hedonic price index system set up by the CBS, and which relies on data collected by the CBS, was established from the beginning of 1995.

Reference population

PINB: Uses a reference population comprising houses or buildings with two or more dwellings built during the reference period in the social rented sector. The required statistical information is obtained through use of building plans and financial documents related to the building contract.

Hedonic price index: Uses the same reference population, but covers the whole low rent residential building sector.

Types of construction covered

PINB: Covers only new residential buildings for the social rented sector, excluding activities linked to repair and maintenance. Within this range the methods used to compile the indices rely on classifications specific to the construction sector such as, by type of works, and by type of component of a standard building. In terms of activities, it does not cover the site preparation (NACE Rev.1 45.1), and repair and maintenance. The coverage falls partly under NACE Rev.1 groups 45.2, 45.3 & 45.4.

Hedonic price index: The coverage of the hedonic price index was extended to the entire low rent residential building construction sector.

Geographic area covered

PINB: One of the criteria used to weight the partial indices used in the composition of the PINB index is the region (North, East, South, and West).

Hedonic price index: Also uses regions as one of the specification components of the econometric model used in this price index method.

The total area covered is the Netherlands.

Items included in the indices

PINB: Shows the evolution of the price of the residential building construction output in the social rented sector. The PINB is constructed by weighting partial price indices corresponding to a number of residential building plans. The partial price indices used in the compilation of the PINB index are weighted according to the number of dwellings in the buildings, and by region.

Wages for architects or quantity surveyors are not included in the prices collected.

Sources of data

PINB: Uses data collected through financial and technical files collected by the Ministry of Public Housing, Planning and Environment.

Hedonic price index: Uses price index data collected by the CBS. The index is based on an exhaustive survey of the reference population.

Method of compilation

PINB: The partial indices used to compile the PINB result from detailed cost-quality evaluation procedures delegated by the Ministry of Public Housing to external certified experts. The procedures consist of filtering out the pure price change of residential building construction by matching a theoretical reference price with the real price observed. Two kinds of prices are available:

- the gross amount specified on the contract for the construction of a residential building selected in the sample; and

- the basic costs of a standard design corresponding to the building constructed.

The gross contract amount is reduced to CBS building costs (approximately 85 per cent of the gross amount) by deducting:

- excessive costs for setting up building sites (1-3 per cent, depending on the region);

- costs for special facilities not included in the standard plan [central heating (5 per cent), sound damping installation (0.2 per cent), or other (1.5 per cent)]; and

- costs pertaining to above standard design quality (6-8 per cent).

The basic costs of the standard design are grossed up to obtain the reference costs by adjusting the price according to:

- the size (in cubic metres) and type of building (single or multi-family buildings);

- the depth and type of foundations (important characteristic depending on the type of soil, including one specific to certain regions of Netherlands where piles are necessary); and

- (dis)economies of scale depending on the size, type, design, and number of dwellings in the building.

The partial index is the ratio of the building costs to the reference costs.

Hedonic price index: Is based on observed real series over the period 1980 to 1991, and the fact that the share of each of the price components described above has either a stable or "explainable" evolution that can be modelled by relating it to observable variables. These variables correspond to the characteristics of the building plans (gross contract amount, size in cubic meters, number of storeys in the building, number of building blocks, number of dwellings, foundation depth, etc.).

Compilation of weights

PINB: The partial indices entering in the composition of the PINB are weighted according to several criteria:

- size of the building in cubic metres;
- type of building (single or multiple dwellings buildings);
- number of dwellings in the building; and
- region.

Type of index, base year and frequency of compilation

PINB: Is compiled monthly according to the Laspeyres formula.

Hedonic price index: Is the result of an hedonic regression calculated monthly.

The base year for both indices is 1995.

Use(s) of the index

The PINB was used in the national accounts to deflate the value of construction output for new residential buildings, and the gross domestic fixed capital formation in residential construction.

This system relied on the fact that social housing once represented a large part of new residential building construction. However, this share has gradually decreased over time to approximately 25 per cent. This is the reason why the coverage of the hedonic price index (which replaced the PINB) was extended to the whole residential building sector.

Publications

Only one series is published corresponding to the low rent residential housing.

The index is published in Price Indices for the Output of New Residential Buildings.

Resume

Three construction price indices are calculated in New Zealand: input price indices covering intermediate consumption (i.e. current purchases excluding labour and capital expenditure); output price indices for the construction industry group measuring changes in the prices of what is produced by businesses predominantly engaged in construction activities; and a capital goods price index which measures price movements in productive capital assets purchased by New Zealand industries.

The methodologies for the output price indices for the construction industry group, and the capital goods price index are described below. The input price indices are described in the this publication under Input Price Indices.

Organisation Responsible for Index

Statistics New Zealand
PO Box 2922
Wellington

Telephone and fax numbers

Tel: (+644) 495 4600

Fax: (+644) 495 4617

Types of construction covered

Output price indices for the construction industry group: Measures movements in the prices of what is produced by businesses predominantly engaged in construction activities. All activities of the construction group are covered in these indices, including non-characteristic activities. For example, if a building company operates a quarry or a freight service and does not keep separate accounts for these activities they are included in the construction indices. Similarly, all work by businesses not predominantly classified to the construction industry are excluded.

New work, repair/renovation work and subcontracting work are included. Intra-industry transactions are not netted out.

Capital goods price index: Covers the full range of construction activity where industries, including central and local government, are the purchaser. The index includes alterations and additions to buildings. Repair work is excluded as this is normally regarded as a current expense. Dwellings purchased for the household sector are excluded.

Items included in the indices

Output price indices for the construction industry group: Includes all those items normally built into the price paid by purchaser of the building to the builder. These include materials, labour, equipment hire, land preparation costs, permits, bathroom, kitchen and outside fittings, professional fees (in some cases), overheads, profits and trade margins.

Value added tax is not included in the prices used in calculation of the indices. Due to practical difficulties the figures are not net of discounts.

Capital goods price index: Measures price movements in produced capital assets purchased by New Zealand industries. It includes a sub-index for buildings and other construction. This represents finished work, but due to practical difficulties most of the pricing is done from specific and generalised models (refer below) rather than by using data on actual finished constructions.

The range of elements included in these models varies according to the nature of the goods purchased. Though not necessarily identified separately in the prices for capital goods purchased, the main components are materials, labour, equipment hire, land preparation costs, fittings, trade margins, overheads and profits, with expenditure on permits and professional fees only included in some cases, since they are often covered by the purchaser rather than the builder.

Taxes are not included in the prices used in calculation of the indices. Due to practical difficulties the figures are not net of discounts.

Sources of data

Output price indices for the construction industry group: Uses data obtained from a variety of sources. Construction and other enterprises are a major direct source, while some data collected in the first instance for use elsewhere in the producers price index are also used for the construction index. Use is also made of the publication *New Zealand Building Economist*, which gives regional estimated prices for installed work.

Capital goods price index: Data used in the compilation of this index are obtained from a variety of sources, normally via a postal commodity price survey of construction and other enterprises. These data are often used in a number of price indices. Extensive use is also made of the publication *New Zealand Building Economist.*

Method of compilation

A number of models and projects are used in the compilation of both types of output indices. Three approaches are taken.

A range of 18 models, derived from schedules of quantities, is repriced each quarter. These models span a wide field, from school and office buildings, to factories, sheds, and a church. Prices for installed work are used together with some material, labour and plant prices.

More generalised models are used for a range of disparate project types, ranging from road and railway construction, water and gas supply, to car park and power line construction, and irrigation schemes. For these most pricing is carried out at the work phase level, e.g. earthworks, metalling, sealing or at the materials/labour/plant level.

Output prices for complete jobs are collected for a smaller number of more easily defined projects, such as well drilling and swimming pool construction.

The list of models and projects used is reviewed at approximately ten-yearly intervals. The projects themselves have mostly not been revised since the early 1980s.

Compilation of weights

The price indices for the various projects that are priced are combined using weights based primarily on the 1984/85 Census of Building and Construction.

Type of index, base year and frequency of compilation

The Laspeyres formula is used for both types of indices.

The indices are calculated quarterly using the fourth quarter of 1989 as a base. For publication, however, the indices are spliced to the standard Producers Price Index expression base of the fourth quarter of 1982 (taken as equal to 1000).

Publications

The index results are published in a variety of outlets including the monthly bulletin *Key Statistics*, the quarterly information release *Hot Off The Press*, and through the on-line system INFOS.

In addition to these outputs indices, details of wage rate movements for the construction industry group are published in the *Labour Cost Index*.

Resume

Statistics Norway has calculated a quarterly construction price index for detached houses (one dwelling building) since 1990. The index is calculated using an hedonic method using multiple regression techniques, and computed according to a Paasche year to year chained formula.

Statistics Norway also calculates monthly construction cost indices for residential buildings and quarterly construction cost indices for civil engineering works. These are described in this publication under Input Price Indices.

Organisation responsible for index

Statistics Norway
Division for Construction and Service Statistics
P.O.B. 1260
N-2201 Kongsvinger

Telephone and fax numbers

Tel: (+47) 62 88 54 64

Fax: (+47) 62 88 54 62

Other organisation involved

The price index is currently financed by the Association of Norwegian Insurance Companies, and is used to regulate the estimated value of residential buildings.

Statistics Norway is responsible for the calculation and publication of the index.

Reference population

The reference population is all detached houses completed in the reference period. Detached houses with less than 50 square metres, or more than 450 square metres of useful floor space are not included. Detached houses with unusually high or low building costs are also excluded.

Types of construction covered

The price index only covers new detached houses. In the last five years, approximately 35-40 per cent of residential dwellings completed were detached houses.

In terms of NACE Rev.1, groups 45.1, 45.2, 45.3 and 45.4 are partly covered, but no breakdown by activity is available.

Geographic area covered

One of the variables used in the multiple regression is geographic location. This distinguishes between Zone 1 (covering Oslo, part of Akershus, Nordland, Troms and Finmark (which is given a heavy weight)), and the rest of the country treated with a dummy variable.

The geographic area covered by the reference population is the whole Norway.

Items included in the indices

The price index does not include site value, or such costs as, connection to road, water and sewer services, duties and administrative fees, and interest on building loans.

The VAT is included in the price calculation.

The variables used in the regression analysis correspond to characteristics that influence the price of detached houses. These comprise: useful floor space, number of rooms, number of bathrooms, number of WCs, number of fireplaces, different types of self-built works, category of housing loan, ground site quality, ventilation and heating systems, sauna, roofing, geographic location, terrace, central vacuum cleaner.

Sources of data

The data for computing the price index are obtained from two different sources: the Ground Property, Address and Building Register (GAB), and a quarterly survey.

The administrative register (GAB) contains information on all ground properties, addresses and buildings in Norway.

The municipalities currently provide the necessary information for the GAB based on data supplied by the responsible client and authorities.

The GAB provides information on dwellings completed during the reference period, and details about the final owner of the building. In addition, the register contains information on classification and quality variables such as, the type of building, location, useful floor space, and quality characteristics that may have an influence on prices.

A questionnaire is distributed quarterly to all investors (final owners) of new detached houses (about 1 500 to 2 000 every quarter in 1995).

Method of compilation

For the quarterly survey, Statistics Norway requests true prices and several quality characteristics. Approximately 65 per cent of the population complete the questionnaire. Quality tests indicate that there are no essential differences between the final sample and the population concerning the floor space and the location of the houses.

Residential buildings (also detached dwellings) vary in size, type, interior and exterior quality, etc. A price index should not be affected by the fact that houses built in different periods differ in quality. In other words a method of "quality purifying" is required. To achieve this objective the so-called hedonic method was applied.

This method is based on the hypothesis that the value of a product is dependant on its attributes and characteristics. Hedonic prices are defined as the implicit value of a product's attributes.

Assuming there are a sufficient number of new detached dwellings sold on the open market, and that the investors are acting rationally, the price of a given dwelling can be related to its attributes, by using a multiplicative regression model.

The quality of the index depends on the quality of the regression model. Two conditions are important: which variables you choose to include in the model, and how the model is specified.

Statistics Norway uses a linear regression equation, with price *(P)* per square metre as the dependent variable. With *X1,.........,Xn* as *n* numerical quality and classification variables, the linear regression model takes the form:

$$P_t = b_{0t} + b_{1t}X_{1t} + \ldots + b_{nt}X_{nt} + \varepsilon_t$$

$$\varepsilon_t = \text{error term}$$

A reason for selecting the price per square metre as dependent variable, instead of the price per dwelling, was the problem of heteroscedasticity. Price variations were found to increase with the size of the dwelling. Floor space had the greatest influence on the variation in house prices.

The relation between the price per square metre and floor space was not found to be linear. The logarithm of floor space gave an approximate linear relation, and less variance for the estimated coefficient.

Most variables in the equation are dummy variables or classification variables. Some variables are not directly linked with the quality standards of the houses but to some extent influence the variations in prices. These are factors such as location, category of housing loans, the extent of "self building" work undertaken by the investor, etc. These variables are treated as dummy variables.

Compilation of weights

Parameter estimates are based on 6 600 observations from 1993 and 1994.

Type of index, base year and frequency of compilation

The price index is computed according to the Paasche formula as a chain index with annual links. This model has computational advantages over the Laspeyres formula because the coefficient *b* need only to be calculated once a year for the base period.

Observations from both the base year and the year before are used in the regression analysis to obtain more confident and stable estimates of the hedonic price functions. The price elasticities *b1.....bk* are assumed to be constant for that period of time.

The base year used for the calculation of the index is 1990=100.

Data are collected, and the index is compiled quarterly.

Publications

The indices are published according to a detailed breakdown by types of work in the monthly construction statistics review *Bygginfo*.

Resume

The Swedish Statistical Office (SCB) calculates a quarterly building price index for new residential buildings using an hedonic price methodology. The index is computed according to a Paasche year to year chained formula. The evaluation of prices is carried out by multiple regression that takes account of the heterogeneous impacts of quality attributes of the houses on prices.

The SCB also calculates a factor price index for the construction industry. The methodology for this index is described in this publication under Input Price Indices.

Organisation responsible for index

Statistiska Centralbyrån SCB (Statistics Sweden)
Karlavägen, 100
Box 24 300
S - 115 81 STOCKHOLM

Telephone and fax numbers

Tel: (+46) 8 783 47 86

Fax: (+46) 8 783 49 05

Reference population

The survey unit is a government aid loan for new construction where the average useful floor space of dwellings is at least 45 square metres or, where the residential primary useful floor space is equal or more than twice the total of non-residential useful floor space, plus accessory space.

Types of construction covered

The building price index covers two categories of new residential buildings: collectively built one or two-dwelling buildings, and multi-dwelling buildings.

Privately financed multi-dwelling buildings (1 per cent of the total), and new dwellings located in mainly non-residential buildings (also 1 per cent of the total) are not covered by the index.

One or two-dwelling buildings built without government aid as well as those financed by a government loan, but individually built (as opposed to collectively) are also not covered by the index.

The index covers 40-65 per cent of one or two dwelling buildings.

NACE Rev.1 groups 45.1, 45.2, 45.3 and 45.4 are partly covered, but no breakdown by activity is available.

Geographic area covered

The building price index is calculated for the whole Sweden.

Items included in the indices

The prices used to compile the building price index correspond to the building prices prevailing at the time of construction, including costs of ground preparation, primary planning, and VAT.

A wide range of items are covered in the calculation of the index. These include the cost of materials (including transport to site); the cost of labour; the cost of permits; the cost of hire; land preparation costs (excluding purchase); installation costs for gas, electricity and telephone (excluding connection fees for water); internal and external fittings; professional fees; interest payable on loans; trade margins, overheads and profits.

Sources of data

The data used to compile the price index are obtained from investors, and from application forms submitted to government authorities to obtain housing aid for new construction.

This information has been recorded on magnetic tapes by Statistics Sweden since 1968 (IDLA-project). The information stored relates to prices and quality characteristics on the stock of houses, as well as structural variables that influence prices.

At the moment, as the reference population is limited, data collection is based on an exhaustive survey. When it exceeds 500 individuals for each type of building the SCB plans to use a stratified sample.

Method of compilation

The building price index is an hedonic index computed on the basis of a regression analysis. The variables used are those that explain the variation in the building prices of different categories of buildings.

The building prices used in the regression calculations are expressed in terms of price per square metre of primary useful floor area (dependent variable).

The regression analysis is based on two sets of explanatory variables that are expressed in a similar way.

The first group corresponds to estimated averages of quality characteristics that influence the price of a building, and assumes that the market prices of newly built buildings are strongly correlated with these quality characteristics. The variables correspond to weighted averages of the values of several kinds of equipment and enclosed areas of walls and roofs. The estimates are derived from calculations of the mortgage value of houses, and are provided by the National Housing Board.

The second group corresponds to structural characteristics that influence the building price, such as geographic location, type of building, the investor's category, and the size of the project.

Type of index, base year and frequency of compilation

The building price index is compiled monthly according to a year to year chained Paasche formula.

The base year is the preceding year.

Use(s) of the index

The index is used for deflation, national accounts, and the consumer price index. It is also used for analysis purposes. The change in productivity and profits can be estimated by comparing the building price index and the factor price index.

Publications

Separate indices are published for multi-dwelling buildings, and for collectively built one or two dwelling buildings.

The index is released in the monthly publication *Byggindex*.

Resume

The Department of Environment in the United Kingdom produces a range of price indices relating to:

- Public sector house building,
- Public sector non house building, and
- Road construction price (new and renovation).

In addition, the Royal Institute of Chartered Surveyors calculates and disseminates quarterly commercial and industrial building indices.

On the basis of these indicators, and new orders data, the DOE derives composite output price indices for the construction sector.

All indices are compiled on the basis of the schedule of prices methodology, except for the public sector housebuilding price index compiled using the component cost method.

Several input construction price indices are also compiled for Great Britain. These are described in this publication under Input Price Indices.

Organisation responsible for index

Department of Environment (DOE)
Construction Market Intelligence Division
2 Marsham Street
LONDON SW1P 3EB

Telephone and fax numbers

Tel: (+44) 1 71 276 47 51

Fax : (+44) 1 71 276 38 26

Other organisation involved

The commercial and industrial building price indices are compiled and disseminated by the Royal Institute of Chartered Surveyors.

Reference population

The reference population is defined in terms of building projects for which the DOE collects the successful tender prices.

The prices correspond to the price offer made by a contractor to take charge of a project. It covers materials (including their transport to the site), labour, equipment hire, land preparation costs, building permits, installation of gas, electricity and water, installations and completion, professional fees (architects, engineers and solicitors), interest on loans, trade margins, overheads and profits.

Types of construction covered

Tender price indices: Different tender price indices are calculated according to the type of building covered. The following breakdown is used:

- Public Sector buildings:
  - New housing (dwellings in blocks of up to 4 storeys)
  - New non-housing (schools, hospitals, prisons, courts, etc.)

- Private Sector buildings:
  - New Commercial buildings
  - New Industrial buildings

- New Road construction

The price indices described here are all based on the collection of prices obtained from bills of quantities attached to one construction project. The bill of quantities details the work to be done in items or services corresponding to type of construction work categories.

A list of well-defined items is proposed in the survey form used for the public sector house building price index. Each of these items is selected to represent all the work in a particular trade section:

The other tender price indices do not use a pre-defined list due to the greater diversity of work in these types of construction.

Output price indices: Separate output price indices are calculated for each of the following:

- New housing:
  - Public housing
  - Private housing

- Other new work:
  - Infrastructure
  - Public non-housing building
  - Private industrial
  - Private commercial

- All new construction.

The price indices cover the main building activities, as well as installations and completion. It does not cover repair and maintenance, alterations and extensions.

The indices follow the same breakdown by type of construction work as the orders received data.

NB: The infrastructure series are estimated on the basis of the road construction tender prices (75 per cent), and the tender prices for industrial buildings (25 per cent). The prices for other types of infrastructure (bridges, sports fields, tunnels, air fields, etc.) are not directly measured.

Geographic area covered

Tender price indices: The scope of the public sector housebuilding tender price index is limited to England and Wales. The public sector non-housing building, and the road construction tender price indices cover England, Scotland and Wales, but not Northern Ireland. The commercial and industrial buildings tender price indices cover the whole United Kingdom.

Output price indices: Cover the same geographic area as the tender price indices from which they are derived.

Items included in the indices

Tender price indices

Public sector housebuilding price index: Provides a measure of the change in tender prices based on the bill of quantities for the successful tenders for dwellings in blocks of up to four storeys built by traditional methods.

Public sector non-housing price index: Measures the movement of prices in competitive tenders for building contracts in the public sector.

Road construction price index: Provides a measure of the change in tender prices based on the bill of quantities of the winning tenders for new contracts with a work cost of £1m or more.

Output price indices

Output price indices measure inflation in the total amount of a particular type of construction being carried out during the reference quarter.

Sources of data

Depending on the index, data are obtained from different sources:

Tender price indices

Public sector housebuilding price index: The data correspond to prices listed in successful tenders for all schemes undertaken for local authorities, and Housing Associations in England and Wales.

Public sector non-house building price index: The main data sources are the Ministry of Defence, Scottish Development Department, Department of Health, Department of Social Security, Home Office, and Department for Education.

Road construction tender price index: Uses data obtained from authorities in charge of the different kinds of road construction. These include the English Department of Transport, the Scottish and the Welsh Offices, county councils, metropolitan districts and London boroughs.

Commercial and industrial building tender price index: Uses data obtained from the members of the Royal Institute of Chartered Surveyors.

Output price indices

Output price indices are derived from the tender price indices mentioned above, and from the new orders indices also compiled by the DOE.

Method of compilation

Tender price indices: Are calculated by analysing bills of quantities, one for each construction project considered. These provide for each item or service (building operations covered by the contract) the contribution (in £s) this operation provides to the total value of the contract. The sum of these contributions equals the total tender price of the project.

These values are converted into quantities and rates to obtain quantifiable items. The rate in £s per unit quantity, for the index base year, is known from a separate exhaustive study carried out in the base year. Thus, for each item in the bill of quantities the actual price and a hypothetical base year price are available.

A Paasche index is then calculated for each project by taking the quotient of the sum for all quantifiable items in the bill of quantities of the actual prices and the sum for the same items of the hypothetical base year price. These project indices are then combined and various smoothing techniques are applied to obtain the published tender price index.

The details of the method for each index are described below.

Output price indices: Are derived from tender price indices, and are used as deflators to convert contractors output of new construction work from current prices to constant prices.

Output of new construction work in a quarter is made up of work done on contracts let during or before that quarter. The deflator can be constructed from the value and volume of orders placed in previous quarters once adjustments have been made to tender prices for changes in materials and labour costs for which reimbursement is allowed under "variation of price" clauses.

The value of orders placed in a given quarter used to estimate the value of output is obtained from the statistics on orders.

The volume of orders is obtained by deflating the value of orders placed in one quarter by the tender price index of this quarter.

The output price index corresponds to the quotient of the value at current price of the work done in quarter T on the basis of contracts placed in quarter T, and in preceding quarters, and the volume of the same work done.

For construction types such as private housing, or various forms of repair and maintenance work, for which the Government has no tender price indices to employ, a mix of material cost indices, and labour cost indices is used instead.

The output price index for private housing is compiled using the method described above with a proxy-tender price index calculated on the basis of:

- house prices at mortgage approval stage (50% of the index);

- house building costs of materials (25%);

- house building labour cost (25%), comprising:
  - 56% of skilled labour,
  - 29% of unskilled labour,
  - 8% of labour on heating and ventilation,
  - 7% of labour on electrical work.

The output price series for infrastructure are based on the road construction tender price index (for 75 per cent), and the tender price for industrial building (for 25 per cent).

Type of index, base year and frequency of compilation

Tender price indices

Public sector housebuilding price index: Is based on the pricing of 21 well defined items selected to represent all the work in a particular trade section. Price movements of work in a trade section are assumed to be broadly similar to those of the representative item.

The index is compiled as a Laspeyres price index in which a weighted arithmetic average of the price relatives is taken for the 21 items for the current quarter in relation to the base year. This method is close to the concept of the standard component method.

Public sector non-house building price index: An index is calculated for each project surveyed by repricing projects at base year rates. Each contract is broken down into disjoint sub-sections, and items amounting to 25 per cent by value are costed within each sub-section. The base period prices are taken from the *Schedule of Rates,* a document published every five years.

The quarterly index is calculated from all the project indices according to the Paasche formula. A simple three point moving average is applied to median values estimated from the project indices for three quarters centred on the reference quarter.

The use of the Paasche formula, rather than the Laspeyres formula as in the housing index, reflects the much greater diversity in these non-housing projects. This method is close to the concept of a schedule of price method.

Road construction tender price index: Entails the calculation of individual project indices according to the Paasche formula. All items included in the bill of quantities are costed for each project. These number around 2 000 items taken across all projects. The base period prices are taken from the *Schedule of Rates,* a document published every five years.

For each quarter, the individual project indices for that quarter, and the 11 past quarters are used to calculate adjustment factors by type of work, size of contract, and region of country. Quarterly medians are obtained from the individual project indices. The medians are transformed (to normality) after being divided by the public sector non-housing price index. The resultant series is smoothed using a Kalman filter, the transformation is reversed and the result multiplied by the public Sector non-housing index to obtain the published index.

This method is close to the concept of schedule of price method.

Commercial and industrial building tender price index: Is calculated on the basis of a Paasche formula according to a method similar to that used for the public sector non-house building price index.

Output price indices

The type of index used is described above under "Method of compilation".

All indices are expressed in base 100=1990.

The following price indices are compiled quarterly:

- Public sector housebuilding tender price index
- Public sector non-house building tender price index
- Road construction tender price index
- All output price indices.

The commercial and industrial tender price indices are calculated monthly.

Use(s) of the index

Tender price indices are used to calculate the output price indices.

The output price indices are used to deflate the contractors' output of new construction work from current prices to constant prices.

Publications

The public sector housebuilding tender price index, the public sector non-housing building tender price index, and the road construction tender price index are published quarterly and annually in:

- Housing and Construction Statistics (DOE);
- through a quarterly subscription service; and
- Quarterly Building Price and Cost Indices (Building Research Establishment).

In addition, for the public sector non-housing building tender price index, separate indices are published by type of contract, fixed price and variation of price contracts, and all-in contracts.

Separate adjustment factors are also published for 36 areas of Great Britain, as well as for 21 different types of building.

The commercial and industrial buildings tender price indices are published together, and as separate series in the monthly bulletin of the Royal Institute's Building Cost Information Service.

Resume

In the United States a variety of cost and price indices are calculated for the construction sector by public and private sector agencies.

Two output construction price indices are compiled. These cover highway construction, and large projects such as dams and power plants.

A seller's price index for new one family houses is also compiled. This is described in this publication under Seller's Price Indices.

Organisations responsible for index

Federal Highway Administration
400 Seventh Street S.W.
Washington D.C. 20590

Bureau of Reclamation
US Department of Interior
Denver, Colorado

Telephone and fax numbers

Federal Highway Administration

Tel: (+202) 366 4636

Bureau of Reclamation

Tel: (+303) 236 6924

Types of construction covered

Highway construction price index: Shows the price trends for Federal-aid highway construction in the United States, and represents the current purchasing power of the Federal-aid construction dollar as measured by six indicator items. The index covers highways, roads and bridges projects with value over USD1.0 million.

Cost index for large projects: Measures construction cost trends for large projects such as dams and power plants.

Geographic area covered

Highway construction price index: Covers total United States.

Cost index for large projects: The indices reflects the Bureau of Reclamation's cost of constructing dams and reclamation projects in eleven western states.

Items included in the indices

Highway construction price index: This index is based on bid prices submitted by contractors at the time of award of the contract. Elements included in the bid prices are materials (including the cost of transportation to the site), labour, equipment hire, land preparation costs, overheads and profits. No tax element is included in the prices, though they do reflect discounts where these are available.

Cost index for large projects: Is calculated as a weighted average of labour, material and equipment costs based on unit costs from contracts let. Elements included in the index are materials (including the cost of their transportation to the site), labour, equipment hire, land purchase costs, the cost of permits, overheads and profits. Taxes and discounts are reflected in the unit prices collected.

Sources of data

Highway construction price index: The data are provided by the State Highway Agencies, which are responsible for the highway construction program. About 1 500 executed contracts are sampled annually.

Cost index for large projects: The data used in the compilation of the index are obtained from various sources, including directly from construction enterprises, from producer price index data sources, and from components of the Federal price index for highway construction.

Bid prices are obtained for common excavation, portland cement, concrete pavement, bituminous concrete pavement, reinforced steel, structural steel, and structural concrete.

The labour costs data used are obtained from the U.S. Department of Labor, and are based on rates set in collective wage agreements. They include social contributions paid by employers.

Method of compilation

Highway construction price index: The index is compiled using data for each sampled project on the cost of six major indicator items (common excavation, Portland cement concrete surfaces, bituminous concrete surfaces, structural reinforcing steel, structural steel , and structural concrete), which together represent about a third of overall project cost.

Average unit cost data for each item are then derived, and weighted together in calculation of the index according to the Laspeyres formula. Data for 1987 was used to determine the weights, on the basis of survey information covering about 35 per cent of output in this construction sector.

Cost index for large projects: The index is calculated as a weighted average of costs based on unit prices. At the basic level calculations are carried out for seven different types of heavy construction project. Unit costs are calculated for 10 to 300 items depending on the nature of the project (e.g. dams, pumping plants, pipelines, etc.).

For the categories of reclamation work included in the index (e.g. dams, pumping plants, canals, hydro-electric power plants, transmission lines, etc.) the basic cost components have been defined and relative weights for each of these components derived from contracts awarded.

All projects owned by the Bureau of Reclamation are examined for index purposes.

Compilation of weights

Highway construction price index: The base for each state is its own particular "market basket" of quantities and costs during the base period. The composite index for each state measures the change in that state's index since the base year. The annual index is a weighted average of the indicator items for the composite index.

Cost index for large projects: What is essentially a Laspeyres methodology is used, with the weights and the types of project that are analysed being reviewed and adjusted periodically by the U.S. Bureau of Reclamation to take account of changes in construction technique, labour efficiencies and labour and material inputs.

Type of index, base year and frequency of compilation

Both indices are calculated quarterly according to the Laspeyres formula.

The highway construction price index has reference base 1987=100, and the cost index for large projects has reference base 1977=100.

Use(s) of index

The indices calculated by Federal agencies are used as deflators of monthly data on the value of construction work done, for the purposes of the Bureau of the Census publication *Value of New Construction Put in Place* (Current Construction Reports (C30)).

Publications

Highway construction price index: The index results are published each quarter in *Price Trends for Federal-Aid Highway Construction* (Publication No. FHWA-PD-94-006). In addition to the aggregate results, separate indices are published for six bid items relating to excavation, paving and structures. Composite index data are available for individual states.

Cost index for large projects: The index results are published each quarter in *Engineers News- Record*.

CANADA

Resume

Seven construction price indices are calculated in Canada. These comprise two output, four input, and one seller's price indices. The seller's price index described below measures changes over time in the contractors' selling prices of new residential houses, where detailed specifications remain the same between two consecutive periods.

The input and output construction price indices are described in this publication under Input Price Indices and Output Price Indices.

No aggregate index combining the seven separate construction price indices is compiled.

Organisation Responsible for Index

Statistics Canada
Jean Talon Building
Tunney's Pasture
Ottawa, Ontario
Canada KIA OT6

Telephone and fax numbers

Tel: (+613) 951 9615

Fax: (+613) 951 2848

Types of construction covered

The new housing index relates to actual completed constructions of private houses. Flats are excluded, as well as condominiums, custom built and self-built houses and rural housing. The index does not measure shelter costs and price changes for existing houses.

Geographic area covered

Price information are collected monthly in 20 metropolitan regions.

Items included in the indices

The prices measured are sale prices, based on contracts, and therefore cover all the costs relating to construction of the property, including those for land purchase and preparation, installation and fitting, architects' and engineers' fees, interest paid by contractors on loans, trade margins, overheads and profits. Basic taxes are not included, nor are notary fees, and real estate agents fees and commissions. However, a separate series including estimated goods and service tax is available. Prices are net of discounts.

Sources of data

About 230 residential building contractors are surveyed each month. The builder providing the data is asked to give, as well as the total price, an estimated price for the land alone, so that the building price can be estimated as a residual.

Interviewers (who also work on the consumer price index) meet the respondents at least quarterly intervals to ensure that data quality is maintained. They also obtain background data on the local market conditions to evaluate the representativeness of the sample.

Method of compilation

The prices are obtained for houses defined by a fixed specification, i.e. matched models are used month-to-month. By its nature this index is self-weighting.

Prices collected relate to the 15th of the month or the nearest business date. The selling prices are adjusted for any changes in quality of the structure and the serviced lot.

Compilation of weights

The sample of builders are given an equal weight in index calculations as are the multiple price reports any given builder might supply. Amongst the cities, weights are obtained from housing completion data.

Type of index, base year and frequency of compilation

The index is calculated monthly using a chain Laspeyres formula.

The index has base year 1986=100 (there are plans to change this to 1992).

Use(s) of index

These indices are used for a variety of purposes, e.g. deflation of construction industry output, deflation of expenditures on gross fixed capital formation, contract escalation, and asset revaluation.

Publications

The index is published monthly in the *Daily Bulletin* and is available quarterly in *Construction Price Statistics* (Cat. No. 62-007). City, regional and provincial indices are available. Indices are available for the total selling price, and also for the structure and land elements separately. Output is available for 20 cities in Canada.

Resume

The collection of data in the construction sector is carried out by the Ministry of Civil Engineering Works (Ministerio de Fomento - formerly MOPTMA: Ministerio de Obras Públicas, Transportes y Medio Ambiente). The average price per square metre of dwellings aims to measure changes over time in the average price of dwellings using information provided by Taxation Societies.

Organisation responsible for index

Ministerio de Fomento
Dirección General de Programación Económica y Presupuestaria
Paseo de la Castellana, 67
E- 28071 Madrid

Telephone and fax numbers

Tel: (+34) 1 597 74 47

Fax: (+34) 1 597 85 24

Population of reference

The reference population is defined in terms of privately built dwellings valued at market prices. Dwellings receiving grants of any type from public or private organisations, or whose values are limited, are excluded.

The reporting units are financial societies that have access by law to the mortgage market.

Types of construction covered

Information only covers completed dwellings, and does not include dwellings built with the help of a subsidy (unless they can be sold at open market prices), dwellings in non-residential buildings, communal residences, and dwellings not yet completed.

Geographical area covered

The indices cover all of Spain.

The NUTS II geographic classification is used.

Items included

The variable monitored is the average price per square metre of dwellings. The price of the dwelling is the open market price as defined by the Ministerial Order of 4 October 1985 (Orden del Ministerio de Economía y Hacienda, fecha 4-X-1985).

Method of compilation

The following information is collected in order to compile the average price of the monitored dwellings:

- date of the valuation
- constructed area (in square metres) of the dwellings
- dwelling price
- age of the dwelling
- postal code and name of the town council where the dwelling is built.

The constructed area is defined in the Ministerial Order of 28 June 1989 (Orden del Ministerio de Economía y Hacienda, fecha 28-VI-1989). It is defined as the useful floor area of the dwelling (total area inside the external walls). The useful floor area includes also 50 per cent of the area of private external spaces (e.g. balconies).

The age of the dwelling is computed from the date it was completed or from the date of the last large redevelopment.

The average price per square metre of dwellings is cross classified by the information from the postal codes database (containing name of the municipality, number of inhabitants, Comunidad Autónoma, etc.) in order to produce results for each stratum: Comunidad Autónoma, geographic area, municipalities size, etc.

Type of index

For each dwelling an average price per square metre is calculated. These average prices are divided by the number of dwellings in each post code to obtain an average price for each post code.

The average price for each town county is then calculated using the weighted mean of the average prices of the different post codes.

The average prices for the Comunidad Autonoma and for the whole country are obtained by aggregating the different town counties indices.

Method of weighting

The weights correspond to the number of inhabitants of the town councils in which the dwellings are located. This information is obtained from the 1992 Population Census.

Type of index, base year and frequency of compilation

Information required to calculate the average prices are obtained from mortgage valuation files available from financial societies that by law have access to the mortgage market. The information is available on tape and is collected quarterly. Prices obtained are published in absolute values (pesetas).

Use(s) of the index

The information is used to monitor housing policy.

Publications

The average price per square metre of dwellings is available for different breakdowns such as:

- average price per size of "Comunidad Autónoma" (region level: NUTS II)

- average price per size of the municipality, of dwellings less than one year old

- average price per size of the municipality, of dwellings more than one year old

- average price per geographical situation of the municipality (in the cost or inside the country)

- average price per homogeneous geographical areas

- average price per age of the dwellings

The average price per square metre of dwellings is published quarterly by the Ministry of Civil Engineering Works (Ministerio de Fomento) in *Boletín estadístico* and annually in the monograph *Precios medios del m2 de las viviendas*.

The information is also available on floppy disk which includes historic information and software to manipulate the data.

The methodology used to compile the average price per square meter of dwellings was published in 1995 in *Boletín estadístico. Notas metodológicas* (ISBN 84-498-0077-3).

Resume

In the United States a variety of cost and price indices are calculated for the construction sector by public and private sector agencies.

A seller's price index for new one family houses is compiled, and is described below.

Two output construction price indices are also compiled. These cover highway construction, and large projects such as dams and power plants. These are described in this publication under Output Price Indices.

Organisation Responsible for Index

Bureau of the Census

Telephone and fax numbers

Tel: (+1) 301 457 4597

Fax: (+1) 301 457 4583

Types of construction covered

This index is designed to measure changes over time in the sales price of new one-family houses which are the same with respect to many important physical characteristics. The index is calculated by the Bureau of the Census, and is based on the hedonic method, with prices for a sample of new privately-built houses being regressed against characteristics of those houses.

Geographic area covered

The price index covers the entire United States.

Items included in the indices

The prices used in this index are actual sale prices of new houses, and as such cover all the elements involved in their construction. The sales prices of the houses exclude taxes.

Sources of data

The sale price data, together with information on the physical characteristics of the houses, are obtained from the Bureau's Housing Sales Survey. The survey collects information on the physical characteristics and the sales prices of new one-family houses sold. This is done through monthly interviews with the builders or owners of a national sample of these houses. About 15 000 houses are included in the sample annually.

Method of compilation

The price index is derived using the hedonic method. Five separate models are used, one for detached houses for each of four regions, and one for attached houses in the country as a whole.

Each of these models is designed to measure changes over time in the sales price of new one-family houses which are the same with respect to many important physical characteristics. Seven characteristics are common to all these models: floor area, geographic division within region, whether inside a metropolitan statistical area, number of fireplaces, number of bathrooms, type of parking facility, and type of foundation. In addition, some further characteristics are used that are specific to individual models.

For each model the index is calculated by making a regression estimate of the logarithm of the sales price against the relevant characteristics, each of the characteristics except floor area being expressed in terms of one or more binary variables.

To give the index for the United States as a whole the indices calculated from the five models are weighted together using as weights the shares of the house types among total houses sold in 1992.

Type of index, base year and frequency of compilation

For most purposes a Paasche version of the index is used, but results calculated according to the Laspeyres formula are also available.

Reference base 1992=100.

The index is calculated monthly, though the published results focus largely on quarterly figures.

Use(s) of index

The indices calculated by Federal agencies are used as deflators of monthly data on the value of construction work done, for the purposes of the Bureau of the Census publication *Value of New Construction Put in Place*.

Publications

The index results are published each month in Bureau of the Census reports *C25, New One-family Houses Sold*, and *C30 , Value of New Construction Put in Place*. As well as aggregate figures, results are published by region, by sold/under construction, and by with/without land.

Detailed information on the computation of the index is given in the fourth quarter 1990 issue of *C27, Price Index of New One-Family Houses Sold*.

Regional data are available primarily for four regions.

SECTION 4. COUNTRY SUMMARY TABLES

Table 1. **Construction Price Indices, OECD and European Union Member Countries**

Main Data Sources Used

Table 1A. **INPUT PRICE Indices**

Country	Index Title	Main Data Sources Used
Australia	Civil Engineering	PPIs; foreign trade indices; pay awards
Austria	Housing and estate building costs index	Industrial wholesale price index; wages survey; collective agreements
	Cost index for road construction	as above
	Cost index for bridge construction	as above
Belgium	Composite construction price index	National index of prices of domestic industrial production
Canada	Residential/Non-residential building input costs	PPIs; collective wage agreements
	Electric utility construction price index	Electric utility company purchase data; labour cost survey of employers
	Telecommunications plant	Purchase records of telecommunication companies
	Construction union wage rates	Details of signed wage agreements from construction association
Denmark	Regulating price index for residential building construction	Cost surveyors; manufacturers
	Regulating price indices for civil engineering works	PPIs; labour agreements; haulage contractors union
Finland	Index of building costs	Construction enterprises; PPIs; manufacturers; employer associations
	Building renovation costs index	as above
France	Building construction sector indices (BT indices)	Professional associations; manufacturers' price lists; government authorities
	Price indices for civil engineering sector (TP indices)	as above
Greece	Input materials for the construction of new residential buildings	Materials suppliers; industry associations; construction contractors
Iceland	Index for privately built apartments	Building materials suppliers; price lists; collective wage agreements; wage surveys
Ireland	Housebuilding cost index	Surveys of construction enterprises
	Wholesale prices index of materials	Surveys of wholesalers
	Capital goods price index	as above
Italy	Costs index for a residential building	Construction contractors associations
	Cost index for a building for industrial use	Construction contractors associations; government organisations
	Cost index for stretches of road	Government organisations responsible for road construction
Japan	Construction price index	Price lists of building materials, input-output tables; collective wage agreements; employer surveys
Mexico	Price index for social housing	Survey of construction enterprises
New Zealand	Input indices for the construction sector	Construction enterprises; PPIs for materials, and regional estimated prices published by *New Zealand. Building Economist*

Country	Index Title	Main Data Sources Used
Norway	Cost indices for residential buildings	Materials suppliers
	Construction cost indices for civil engineering works	Existing indices; government agencies
Portugal	Construction cost indices	PPIs; Indices compiled by the Ministry of Qualification and Employment
Spain	Construction cost index	PPIs; provincial collective wage agreements
Sweden	Factor price index for residential buildings	Surveys of construction materials suppliers; current collective wage agreements
	Factor price indices for repair and maintenance of multi-dwelling, and agricultural buildings	Investors; government aid application forms
Turkey	Building construction cost index	Surveys of construction enterprises and materials suppliers
United Kingdom	Construction materials cost index	Professional associations; PPIs
	Construction industry price index of average earnings	as above

Table 1B. **OUTPUT PRICE Indices**

Country	Index Title	Main Data Sources Used
Australia	Construction and renovation of privately built houses	Survey of project home builders; real estate organisations
	Construction of other dwellings and other buildings	Materials suppliers; pay awards; government cost indices
Austria	Residential buildings price indices	Building companies
	Other building price indices	Building companies
	Output price index for road construction	Provincial construction departments; construction companies
	Output price index for bridge construction	as above
	Other civil engineering work	as above
Canada	Apartment building construction	Survey of construction enterprises; PPIs
	Non-residential building construction price index	as above
France	Construction price indices for residential buildings (ICC)	Building permits; client financial and technical documents
Germany	Conventional construction price indices	Surveys of construction contractors
	Standard house price indices	as above
Greece	Work categories for the construction of new residential buildings	Surveys of construction enterprises and contractors
Luxembourg	Price index for the construction of residential and semi residential building	Survey of construction enterprises
Netherlands	Price indices for social rented housing	Housing ministries
	Hedonic price index for the low rent residential building sector	as above
New Zealand	Output index for the construction sector	Construction enterprises; PPIs for materials and regional estimated prices published by N.Z. Building Economist
	Capital goods price index for the construction sector	as above
Norway	Construction price index for detached houses	Surveys of investors
Sweden	Output price indices for houses and apartments	Regression coefficients
Turkey	Building construction cost index	Surveys of construction enterprises and materials suppliers
United Kingdom	Public sector housebuilding price index	Local authorities; relevant ministries
	Public sector non-housing price index	as above
	Road construction tender price index	as above
	Commercial and industrial building tender price index	Professional associations
United States	Price index for highway construction	State highway agencies
	Cost index for large projects	Surveys of construction enterprises; PPIs; government agencies

128

Table 1C. **SELLER'S PRICE Indices**

Country	Index Title	Main Data Sources Used
Canada	New housing price index	Survey of residential building contractors
Spain	Average prices of dwellings per square meters	Local government agencies; financing organisations
United States	Price index for new one family houses	Surveys of house builders and owners of new houses

Table 2. Construction Price Indices, OECD and European Union Member Countries
Methods for Deriving Weights

Table 2A. INPUT PRICE Indices

Country	Index Title	Derivation of Weights
Australia	Civil Engineering	Information from government agencies on expenditure on most significant expenditure items.
Austria	Housing and estate building costs index	Expenditure components of a number of representative construction projects.
	Cost index for road construction	as above
	Cost index for bridge construction	as above
Belgium	Composite construction price index	Selection of items weighted on percentage of construction sectors total inputs in 1980.
Canada	Residential/Non-residential building input costs	Residential buildings based on survey of inputs for building contractors. Non-residential buildings based on analysis of input-output tables.
	Electric utility construction price index	Based on expenditure on utility construction over eight year period.
	Telecommunications plant	Input expenditures based on annual surveys of carriers.
Denmark	Regulating price index for residential building construction	Cost analysis of model residential building.
	Regulating price indices for civil engineering works	Based on standard civil engineering projects.
Finland	Index of building costs	Derived from proportion of expenditure on five building types.
France	Building construction sector indices (BT indices)	Weights of inputs based on proportion of total expenditure on building projects in base year.
	Price indices for civil engineering sector (TP indices)	as above
Greece	Input materials for the construction of new residential buildings	Weights based on analysis of the accounts of a small sample of building enterprises.
Iceland	Index for privately built apartments	Weights derived from cost analyses of finished residential building constructions in base year.
Ireland	Housebuilding cost index	Weights based on model house construction in base year.
	Wholesale prices index of materials	Weights based on analysis of costs reported by building enterprises in construction census.
Italy	Costs index for a residential building	Weights based on the value of housing investments redistributed by products using the shares in total construction of a region in the base year
	Cost index for a building for industrial use	As above with investments in the non - residential building sector
	Cost index for stretches of road	Weights based on cost analysis in the base year
Japan	Construction price index	Weights based on analysis of input-output tables in base year.
Mexico	Price index for social housing	Weights based on cost analysis of model apartment building.
New Zealand	Input index for the construction sector	Weights based on a small number of construction models and on the census of building construction.

Country	Index Title	Derivation of Weights
Norway	Cost indices for residential buildings	Weights based on cost analysis of sample of completed buildings.
	Construction cost indices for civil engineering works	Weights based on specifications from national road authority.
Portugal	Construction Cost Indices	Fixed weights established by financial authorities.
Spain	Construction cost index	Weights based on structural data enquiry conducted in base year.
Sweden	Factor price index for residential buildings	Weights are derived from housing cost studies conducted in base year.
	Factor price indices for repair and maintenance of multi-dwelling, and agricultural buildings	as above
Turkey	Building construction cost index	Weights based on analysis of bills of quantities of a representative sample of construction projects.
United Kingdom	Construction materials cost index	Weights based on a cost analysis of construction work in progress in the base year.
	Construction industry price index of average earnings	as above

Table 2B. OUTPUT PRICE Indices

Country	Index Title	Derivation of Weights
Australia	Construction and renovation of privately built houses	Matched models are equi-weighted.
	Construction of other dwellings and other buildings	Based on bills of quantities for model projects.
Austria	Residential buildings price indices	Expenditure components of a number of representative construction projects.
	Other building price indices	as above
	Output price index for road construction	as above
	Output price index for bridge construction	as above
	Other civil engineering work	as above
Canada	Apartment building construction	Cost analysis of model apartment building
	Non-residential building construction price index	Cost analysis of model non-residential buildings
France	Construction price indices for residential buildings (ICC)	Current weights are based on size and type of residential building.
Germany	Conventional construction price indices	Weights derived on analysis of billing and invoices for given structures built in base year.
Greece	Work categories for the construction of new buildings	Weights based on analysis of the accounts of a small sample of building enterprises.
Luxembourg	Price index for the construction of residential and semi residential building	Weights based on cost analysis of standard model building.
Netherlands	Price indices for social rented housing	Weights based on several characteristics observed in the base year: volume, type of building, number of dwellings and region
	Hedonic price index for the low rent residential building sector	Regression coefficients based on long time series that relate the price components to characteristics of the building constructed..
New Zealand	Output index for the construction sector	Weights based on a small number of construction models.
	Capital goods price index for the construction sector	as above
Norway	Construction price index for detached houses	Regression parameters estimated from 6 600 observations over a two year reference period.
Sweden	Output price indices for houses and apartments	Regression co-efficients estimated from the calculation of mortgage values.
United Kingdom	Public sector housebuilding price index	Separate exhaustive study of tender prices carried out in the base year.
	Public sector non-housing price index	as above
	Road construction tender price index	as above
	Commercial and industrial building tender price index	as above
United States	Price index for highway construction	Weights are derived from an analysis of costs of a sample highway construction projects in base year.

Table 2C. **SELLER'S PRICE Indices**

Country	Index Title	Derivation of Weights
Canada	New housing price index	Houses priced are equi-weighted.
Spain	Average prices of dwellings per square meters	Weights based on the number of inhabitants of the town area where the building is constructed. Information based on the last population census.
United States	Cost index for large projects	Weights are derived from an analysis of costs of a sample of projects in base year.

SECTION 5. INTERNATIONAL CLASSIFICATIONS RELEVANT TO THE COMPILATION OF CONSTRUCTION PRICE INDICES

A. International Standard Industrial Classification (ISIC), Rev. 3

ISIC is a classification of productive economic activities. Its main use is to classify economic entities according to the type of economic activity they carry out. The activity carried out by an entity is the type of production in which it engages.

Tabulation Category	Division	Group	Class
F. Construction	45. Construction	451. Site preparation	4510. Site preparation
		452. Building of complete constructions or parts thereof; civil engineering	4520. Building of complete constructions or parts thereof; civil engineering
		453. Building installation	4530. Building installation
		454. Building completion	4540. Building completion
		455. Renting of construction or demolition equipment with operator	4550. Renting of construction or demolition equipment with operator

B. Statistical Classification of Economic Activities in the European Community (NACE) Rev.1

Section	Division	Group	Class
F. Construction	45. Construction	451. Site preparation	4511. Demolition and wrecking of buildings; earth moving
			4512. Test drilling and boring
		452. Building of complete constructions or parts thereof; civil engineering	4521. General construction of buildings and civil engineering works
			4522. Erection of roof coverings and frames
			4523. Construction of highways, roads, airfields and sports facilities
			4524. Construction of water projects
			4525. Other construction work involving special trades
		453. Building installation	4531. Installation of electrical wiring and fittings
			4532. Insulation work activities
			4533. Plumbing
			4534. Other building installation
		454. Building completion	4541. Plastering
			4542. Joinery installation
			4543. Floor and wall covering
			4544. Painting and glazing
			4545. Other building completion
		455. Renting of construction or demolition equipment with operator	4550. Renting of construction or demolition equipment with operator

C. Provisional Central Product Classification (CPC)

The CPC is a product classification covering goods and services. The main purpose of the classification is to provide a general framework for international comparisons of data from various types of statistics that present data by kinds of product.

The classification comprises Sections, Divisions, Groups, Classes, and Sub-classes. The first four levels are provided below.

Section	Division	Group	Class
5. Construction Work and Constructions: Land	51. Construction work	511. Pre-erection work at construction sites	5111. Site investigation work
			5112. Demolition work
			5113. Site formation and clearance work
			5114. Excavating and earthmoving work
			5115. Site preparation work for mining
			5116. Scaffolding work
		512. Construction work for buildings	5121. For one and two dwelling buildings
			5122. For multi dwelling buildings
			5123. For warehouses and industrial buildings
			5124. For commercial buildings
			5125. For public entertainment buildings
			5126. For hotel, restaurant and similar buildings
			5127. For educational buildings
			5128. For health buildings
			5129. For other buildings
		513. Construction work for civil engineering	5131. For highways, streets, roads, railways, and airfield runways
			5132. For bridges, elevated highways, tunnels and subways
			5133. For waterways, harbours, dams and other water works
			5134. For long distance pipelines, communication and power lines
			5135. For local pipelines and cables; ancillary works
			5136. For constructions for mining and manufacturing

Section	Division	Group	Class
			5137. For constructions for sport and recreation
			5139. For engineering works n.e.c.
		514. Assembly and erection of prefabricated constructions	5140. Assembly and erection of prefabricated constructions
		515. Special trade construction work	5151. Foundation work
			5152. Water well drilling
			5153. Roofing and water proofing
			5154. Concrete work
			5155. Steel bending and erection
			5156. Masonry work
			5159. Other special trade construction work
		516. Installation work	5161. Heating, ventilation and air conditioning work
			5162. Water plumbing and drain laying work
			5163. Gas fitting construction work
			5164. Electrical work
			5165. Insulation work
			5166. Fencing and railing construction work n.e.c.
			5169. Other installation work
		517. Building completion and finishing work	5171. Glazing work and window glass installation work
			5172. Plastering work
			5173. Painting work
			5174. Floor and wall tiling work
			5175. Other floor laying, wall covering and wall papering work
			5176. Wood and metal joinery and carpentry work
			5177. Interior fitting decoration work
			5178. Ornamentation fitting work
			5179. Other building completion and finishing work

Section	Division	Group	Class
		518. Renting services related to equipment for construction or demolition of buildings or civil engineering works, with operator	5180. Renting services related to equipment for construction or demolition of buildings or civil engineering works, with operator
	52. Constructions	521. Buildings	5211. Residential buildings
			5212. Non-residential buildings
		522. Civil engineering works	5221. Highways, streets, roads, railways, airfield runways
			5222. Bridges, elevated highways, tunnels and subways
			5223. Waterways, harbours, dams, and other waterworks
			5224. Long distance pipelines, communication and power lines
			5225. Local pipelines and cables; ancillary works
			5226. Constructions for mining and manufacture
			5227. Constructions for sport and recreation
			5229. Other civil engineering works

D. Classification of Types of Constructions

The draft classification, developed by EUROSTAT consists of 2 Sections, 6 Divisions, 20 Groups, and 47 Classes. The first three levels are listed below.

The classification has been developed on the basis of the CPC published in 1991 by the United Nations.

1. Buildings	11. Residential buildings	111. One-dwelling buildings 112. Two-and more dwelling buildings 113. Residences for communities
	12. Non-residential buildings	121. Hotels and similar buildings 122. Office buildings 123. Wholesale and retail trade buildings 124. Traffic and communication buildings 125. Industrial buildings and warehouses 126. Buildings for public entertainment, education or hospital and institutional care 127. Other non-residential buildings
2. Civil Engineering Works	21. Transport infrastructure	211. Highways, streets and roads 212. Railways 213. Airfield runways 214. Bridges, elevated highways, tunnels and subways 215. Harbours, waterways, dams and other waterworks
	22. Pipelines, communication and electricity lines	221. Long-distance pipelines, communication and electricity lines 222. Local pipelines and cables
	23. Complex constructions on industrial sites	230. Complex constructions on industrial sites (e.g. powerplants, chemical plants, mining constructions)
	24. Other civil engineering works	241. Sport and recreation constructions 242. Other civil engineering works

BIBLIOGRAPHY

- Australian Bureau of Statistics, Canberra - *House Price Indices: Eight Capital Cities* (ABS Cat. No. 6416.0)

- Austrian Central Statistical Office, Vienna, Statistische Nachrichten - *Index of Building Prices*

- Central Bureau of Statistics Netherlands, Voorburg - *A Hedonic Approach to Output Indices for Construction*, George van Leeuwen, February 1995

- EUROSTAT, Luxembourg, Statistical Classification of Economic Activities in the European Community (NACE) Rev.1, 1996

- EUROSTAT, Luxembourg, draft *Classification of Types of Constructions*, February 1996

- EUROSTAT, Luxembourg, *Industrial Trends: National Methods,* Supp. December 1995

- EUROSTAT, Luxembourg, Methodological Aspects of Construction Price Indices, 1996.

- EUROSTAT, Luxembourg, Methodology of Industrial Short Term Indicators - Rules and Recommendations, 1996

- EUROSTAT, Luxembourg, Monalisa: Methods of National Statistical Offices Concerning Industrial Short Term Indicators, electronic reference database on methodology - Unit D2.

- Federal Highway Administration, Washington D.C. - *FHWA Bid Price Index - 1984 Base year,* C.A. Leonin, 1989

- German Federal Statistical Office, Wiesbaden, Studies on Statistics, No. 10 - Comments on the Revision of Statistics on Construction Prices, November 1959

- German Federal Statistical Office, Wiesbaden, *Detailed Indices for Construction Prices and Constructio Work*, Series 4, May 1994

- International Labour Organisation, International Standard Classifications of Occupations (ISCO), 1968-1990

- Institut National de la Statistique et des Etudes Economiques (INSEE), Paris, *Bloc-Notes*

- *4/1990 - France's Cost of Construction Index*, Vincent le Calonnec, 1990

- OECD, Paris, Consumer Price Indices, Sources and Methods, 1994

- OECD, Paris, Main Economic Indicators, Sources and Methods, 1996

- OECD, Paris, Producer Price Indices, Sources and Methods, 1994

- Statistics Canada, Ottawa, *Construction Price Statistics*, (Cat. No. 62-007), quarterly

- Statistics Canada, Ottawa, *Guide to the Income and Expenditure Accounts*, (Cat. No. 13-603E, No.1), occasional, 1990

- United Nations Statistical Office, New York, UN Statistical Papers, Series M, No. 59 - *Guidelines on Principles of a System of Price and Quantity Statistics*

- United Nations Statistical Office, New York, UN Statistical Papers, Series M, No. 64 - *Manual on National Accounts at Constant Prices,* 1979

- United Nations Statistical Office, New York, UN Statistical Papers, Series M, No. 66 - *Manual on Producers' Price Indices for Industrial Goods,* 1979

- United Nations Statistical Office, New York, UN Statistical Papers, Series M, No. 69 - *Strategies for Price and Quantity Measurement in External Trade,* 1981

- United Nations Statistical Office, New York, UN Statistical Papers, Series M. No. 77 - *Provisional Central Product Classification (CPC)*, 1991

- United Nations Statistical Office, New York, UN Statistical Papers, Series M. No. 4 - *International Standard Industrial Classification of All Economic Activities (ISIC), Rev. 3*, 1990

- University of Geneva, Laboratory of Applied Economics, Geneva - *Indices of Construction Prices, A Methodological Inventory*, Lynn Mackenzie, April 1994

Buildings

Buildings are permanently constructed roofed structures capable of being used independently, designed to offer protection from the elements with a view to occupation by humans, or to provide shelter for animals, goods, equipment, or industrial activities.

Building Sector

Comprises the subset of activities within Division 45 of the International Standard Industrial Classification of All Economic Activities, Rev. 3 (ISIC), and Division 45 of the NACE, Rev. 1 contributing to the construction of buildings. Includes building repair and maintenance works.

Civil engineering sector

Comprises the subset of activities within Division 45 of the International Standard Industrial Classification of All Economic Activities, Rev. 3 (ISIC), and Division 45 of the NACE, Rev. 1 contributing to the construction of civil engineering works includes building repair and maintenance of such works.

Civil engineering structures

All structures other than buildings: infrastructure works such as railways, highways, airport runways, tunnels, dams, bridges, canals, electricity transmission systems, drilling platforms, mine shafts, recreation installations, etc.

Client (Maitre d'ouvrage)

Natural or legal person for whom a structure is constructed, or alternatively the person or organisation that took the initiative of the construction.

Contractor

A firm which undertakes works as part of a construction project by virtue of a contract with a client.

Construction

"Construction" is deemed to mean an item connected with the ground, made from construction materials and components, and/or for which construction work is carried out. The classification of constructions [?] provides for two types of such structures: buildings and civil engineering structures.

Construction industry

Refers to all economic activities within Division 45 of the International Standard Industrial Classification of all Economic Activities, Rev. 3 (ISIC), and Division 45 of the NACE, Rev. 1. These activities comprise site preparation, construction of building or civil engineering structures, installation and finishing works, and the hire of construction plant and equipment with operator. It also comprises new works, as well as repair and maintenance works.

Dwellings

A dwelling is deemed to be one or more rooms plus annexes, within a building whose design and manner of construction, reconstruction, alteration, etc. make it suitable for use as a private residence. It should possess its own entrance giving access, directly across a garden or land, to a road or to a thoroughfare within a building (staircase, corridor, gallery, etc.). Isolated rooms manifestly constructed, reconstructed, altered, etc. to form part of a dwelling are included within that dwelling.

Final owner

This is the person or organisation that pays the final seller's price. In some instances, this person or organisation may be the same as the client (refer above).

Habitable floor area

This is the total floor area of the rooms meeting the definition of "room" provided below.

Input price indices

Measure changes in the price of inputs to the construction process by monitoring separately the cost of each factor. This generally entails the compilation of a weighted index of the costs of wages and materials.

Non-residential buildings

Any building of which more than 50 per cent of the useful floor area is used for purposes other than residential.

Output price indices

Measure changes in the prices of what is produced by entities engaged in construction activity.

Project supervisor (Maitre d'oeuvre)

The person or organisation responsible for the supervision of a construction site after having drawn up the structure plans.

Purchaser

This is the person or organisation that pays the final seller's price. In some instances, this person or organisation may be the same as the client (refer above).

Quantity surveyor

Profession responsible for evaluating the progress of work in terms of quality and value, on the basis of the technical documents relating to a given structure.

Residential buildings

Any building of which more than 50 per cent of the useful floor area is used for residential purposes.

Room

A room is an area within a dwelling formed by partition walls from floor to ceiling or roof. It must be large enough to accommodate an adult's bed (not less than 4 square metres) with not less than 2 metres headroom over half its floor area. This includes normal bedrooms, dining rooms, sitting rooms, attic rooms, kitchens, and other separate rooms whose purpose is residential. "Corner-kitchens", corridors, verandas, hallways, etc. and bathrooms do not count as rooms.

Seller's price indices

Measure changes in the prices of construction output paid by the purchaser or final owner of the output of construction activity.

Standard operations

The supply of a component of the structure defined in terms of its function in the structure and its constituent materials. Examples might include:

- Construction of 50 square metres of wall in 20 cm hollow breeze block

- Supply and setting of 60 square metres traditional pantile roofing

- Installation of an insulated 200-litre electric hot water tank

Useful floor area

This is the floor area of a building measured within the external walls, excluding cellars, non-habitable attics, and in multiple dwellings, all communal areas.

MAIN SALES OUTLETS OF OECD PUBLICATIONS
PRINCIPAUX POINTS DE VENTE DES PUBLICATIONS DE L'OCDE

AUSTRALIA – AUSTRALIE
D.A. Information Services
648 Whitehorse Road, P.O.B 163
Mitcham, Victoria 3132   Tel. (03) 9210.7777
                             Fax: (03) 9210.7788

AUSTRIA – AUTRICHE
Gerold & Co.
Graben 31
Wien I   Tel. (0222) 533.50.14
                             Fax: (0222) 512.47.31.29

BELGIUM – BELGIQUE
Jean De Lannoy
Avenue du Roi, Koningslaan 202
B-1060 Bruxelles   Tel. (02) 538.51.69/538.08.41
                             Fax: (02) 538.08.41

CANADA
Renouf Publishing Company Ltd.
5369 Canotek Road
Unit 1
Ottawa, Ont. K1J 9J3   Tel. (613) 745.2665
                             Fax: (613) 745.7660

Stores:
71 1/2 Sparks Street
Ottawa, Ont. K1P 5R1   Tel. (613) 238.8985
                             Fax: (613) 238.6041

12 Adelaide Street West
Toronto, QN M5H 1L6   Tel. (416) 363.3171
                             Fax: (416) 363.5963

Les Éditions La Liberté Inc.
3020 Chemin Sainte-Foy
Sainte-Foy, PQ G1X 3V6   Tel. (418) 658.3763
                             Fax: (418) 658.3763

Federal Publications Inc.
165 University Avenue, Suite 701
Toronto, ON M5H 3B8   Tel. (416) 860.1611
                             Fax: (416) 860.1608

Les Publications Fédérales
1185 Université
Montréal, QC H3B 3A7   Tel. (514) 954.1633
                             Fax: (514) 954.1635

CHINA – CHINE
Book Dept., China National Publiations
Import and Export Corporation (CNPIEC)
16 Gongti E. Road, Chaoyang District
Beijing 100020   Tel. (10) 6506-6688 Ext. 8402
                             (10) 6506-3101

CHINESE TAIPEI – TAIPEI CHINOIS
Good Faith Worldwide Int'l. Co. Ltd.
9th Floor, No. 118, Sec. 2
Chung Hsiao E. Road
Taipei   Tel. (02) 391.7396/391.7397
                             Fax: (02) 394.9176

**CZECH REPUBLIC –
RÉPUBLIQUE TCHÈQUE**
National Information Centre
NIS – prodejna
Konviktská 5
Praha 1 – 113 57   Tel. (02) 24.23.09.07
                             Fax: (02) 24.22.94.33
E-mail: nkposp@dec.niz.cz
Internet: http://www.nis.cz

DENMARK – DANEMARK
Munksgaard Book and Subscription Service
35, Nørre Søgade, P.O. Box 2148
DK-1016 København K   Tel. (33) 12.85.70
                             Fax: (33) 12.93.87

J. H. Schultz Information A/S,
Herstedvang 12,
DK – 2620 Albertslung   Tel. 43 63 23 00
                             Fax: 43 63 19 69

Internet: s-info@inet.uni-c.dk

EGYPT – ÉGYPTE
The Middle East Observer
41 Sherif Street
Cairo   Tel. (2) 392.6919
                             Fax: (2) 360.6804

FINLAND – FINLANDE
Akateeminen Kirjakauppa
Keskuskatu 1, P.O. Box 128
00100 Helsinki

Subscription Services/Agence d'abonnements :
P.O. Box 23
00100 Helsinki   Tel. (358) 9.121.4403
                             Fax: (358) 9.121.4450

*FRANCE
OECD/OCDE
Mail Orders/Commandes par correspondance :
2, rue André-Pascal
75775 Paris Cedex 16   Tel. 33 (0)1.45.24.82.00
                      Fax: 33 (0)1.49.10.42.76
                      Telex: 640048 OCDE
Internet: Compte.PUBSINQ@oecd.org

Orders via Minitel, France only/
Commandes par Minitel, France exclusivement :
36 15 OCDE

OECD Bookshop/Librairie de l'OCDE :
33, rue Octave-Feuillet
75016 Paris   Tel. 33 (0)1.45.24.81.81
                            33 (0)1.45.24.81.67

Dawson
B.P. 40
91121 Palaiseau Cedex   Tel. 01.89.10.47.00
                             Fax: 01.64.54.83.26

Documentation Française
29, quai Voltaire
75007 Paris   Tel. 01.40.15.70.00

Economica
49, rue Héricart
75015 Paris   Tel. 01.45.78.12.92
                             Fax: 01.45.75.05.67

Gibert Jeune (Droit-Économie)
6, place Saint-Michel
75006 Paris   Tel. 01.43.25.91.19

Librairie du Commerce International
10, avenue d'Iéna
75016 Paris   Tel. 01.40.73.34.60

Librairie Dunod
Université Paris-Dauphine
Place du Maréchal-de-Lattre-de-Tassigny
75016 Paris   Tel. 01.44.05.40.13

Librairie Lavoisier
11, rue Lavoisier
75008 Paris   Tel. 01.42.65.39.95

Librairie des Sciences Politiques
30, rue Saint-Guillaume
75007 Paris   Tel. 01.45.48.36.02

P.U.F.
49, boulevard Saint-Michel
75005 Paris   Tel. 01.43.25.83.40

Librairie de l'Université
12a, rue Nazareth
13100 Aix-en-Provence   Tel. 04.42.26.18.08

Documentation Française
165, rue Garibaldi
69003 Lyon   Tel. 04.78.63.32.23

Librairie Decitre
29, place Bellecour
69002 Lyon   Tel. 04.72.40.54.54

Librairie Sauramps
Le Triangle
34967 Montpellier Cedex 2   Tel. 04.67.58.85.15
                             Fax: 04.67.58.27.36

A la Sorbonne Actual
23, rue de l'Hôtel-des-Postes
06000 Nice   Tel. 04.93.13.77.75
                             Fax: 04.93.80.75.69

GERMANY – ALLEMAGNE
OECD Bonn Centre
August-Bebel-Allee 6
D-53175 Bonn   Tel. (0228) 959.120
                             Fax: (0228) 959.12.17

GREECE – GRÈCE
Librairie Kauffmann
Stadiou 28
10564 Athens   Tel. (01) 32.55.321
                             Fax: (01) 32.30.320

HONG-KONG
Swindon Book Co. Ltd.
Astoria Bldg. 3F
34 Ashley Road, Tsimshatsui
Kowloon, Hong Kong   Tel. 2376.2062
                             Fax: 2376.0685

HUNGARY – HONGRIE
Euro Info Service
Margitsziget, Európa Ház
1138 Budapest   Tel. (1) 111.60.61
                             Fax: (1) 302.50.35
E-mail: euroinfo@mail.matav.hu
Internet: http://www.euroinfo.hu//index.html

ICELAND – ISLANDE
Mál og Menning
Laugavegi 18, Pósthólf 392
121 Reykjavik   Tel. (1) 552.4240
                             Fax: (1) 562.3523

INDIA – INDE
Oxford Book and Stationery Co.
Scindia House
New Delhi 110001   Tel. (11) 331.5896/5308
                         Tel. (11) 332.2639
E-mail: oxford.publ@axcess.net.in

17 Park Street
Calcutta 700016   Tel. 240832

INDONESIA – INDONÉSIE
Pdii-Lipi
P.O. Box 4298
Jakarta 12042   Tel. (21) 573.34.67
                             Fax: (21) 573.34.67

IRELAND – IRLANDE
Government Supplies Agency
Publications Section
4/5 Harcourt Road
Dublin 2   Tel. 661.31.11
                             Fax: 475.27.60

ISRAEL – ISRAËL
Praedicta
5 Shatner Street
P.O. Box 34030
Jerusalem 91430   Tel. (2) 652.84.90/1/2
                             Fax: (2) 652.84.93

R.O.Y. International
P.O. Box 13056
Tel Aviv 61130   Tel. (3) 546 1423
                             Fax: (3) 546 1442
E-mail: royil@netvision.net.il

Palestinian Authority/Middle East:
INDEX Information Services
P.O.B. 19502
Jerusalem   Tel. (2) 627.16.34
                             Fax: (2) 627.12.19

ITALY – ITALIE
Libreria Commissionaria Sansoni
Via Duca di Calabria, 1/1
50125 Firenze   Tel. (055) 64.54.15
                             Fax: (055) 64.12.57
E-mail: licosa@ftbcc.it

Via Bartolini 29
20155 Milano   Tel. (02) 36.50.83

Editrice e Libreria Herder
Piazza Montecitorio 120
00186 Roma   Tel. 679.46.28
                             Fax: 678.47.51

Libreria Hoepli
Via Hoepli 5
20121 Milano   Tel. (02) 86.54.46
                             Fax: (02) 805.28.86

Libreria Scientifica
Dott. Lucio de Biasio 'Aeiou'
Via Coronelli, 6
20146 Milano   Tel. (02) 48.95.45.52
                                 Fax: (02) 48.95.45.48

JAPAN – JAPON
OECD Tokyo Centre
Landic Akasaka Building
2-3-4 Akasaka, Minato-ku
Tokyo 107   Tel. (81.3) 3586.2016
                                 Fax: (81.3) 3584.7929

KOREA – CORÉE
Kyobo Book Centre Co. Ltd.
P.O. Box 1658, Kwang Hwa Moon
Seoul   Tel. 730.78.91
                                 Fax: 735.00.30

MALAYSIA – MALAISIE
University of Malaya Bookshop
University of Malaya
P.O. Box 1127, Jalan Pantai Baru
59700 Kuala Lumpur
Malaysia   Tel. 756.5000/756.5425
                                 Fax: 756.3246

MEXICO – MEXIQUE
OECD Mexico Centre
Edificio INFOTEC
Av. San Fernando no. 37
Col. Toriello Guerra
Tlalpan C.P. 14050
Mexico D.F.   Tel. (525) 528.10.38
                                 Fax: (525) 606.13.07
E-mail: ocde@rtn.net.mx

NETHERLANDS – PAYS-BAS
SDU Uitgeverij Plantijnstraat
Externe Fondsen
Postbus 20014
2500 EA's-Gravenhage   Tel. (070) 37.89.880
Voor bestellingen: Fax: (070) 34.75.778

Subscription Agency/   Agence d'abonnements :
SWETS & ZEITLINGER BV
Heereweg 347B
P.O. Box 830
2160 SZ Lisse   Tel. 252.435.111
                                 Fax: 252.415.888

NEW ZEALAND – NOUVELLE-ZÉLANDE
GPLegislation Services
P.O. Box 12418
Thorndon, Wellington   Tel. (04) 496.5655
                                 Fax: (04) 496.5698

NORWAY – NORVÈGE
NIC INFO A/S
Ostensjoveien 18
P.O. Box 6512 Etterstad
0606 Oslo   Tel. (22) 97.45.00
                                 Fax: (22) 97.45.45

PAKISTAN
Mirza Book Agency
65 Shahrah Quaid-E-Azam
Lahore 54000   Tel. (42) 735.36.01
                                 Fax: (42) 576.37.14

PHILIPPINE – PHILIPPINES
International Booksource Center Inc.
Rm 179/920 Cityland 10 Condo Tower 2
HV dela Costa Ext cor Valero St.
Makati Metro Manila   Tel. (632) 817 9676
                                 Fax: (632) 817 1741

POLAND – POLOGNE
Ars Polona
00-950 Warszawa
Krakowskie Prezdmiescie 7   Tel. (22) 264760
                                 Fax: (22) 265334

PORTUGAL
Livraria Portugal
Rua do Carmo 70-74
Apart. 2681
1200 Lisboa   Tel. (01) 347.49.82/5
                                 Fax: (01) 347.02.64

SINGAPORE – SINGAPOUR
Ashgate Publishing
Asia Pacific Pte. Ltd
Golden Wheel Building, 04-03
41, Kallang Pudding Road
Singapore 349316   Tel. 741.5166
                                 Fax: 742.9356

SPAIN – ESPAGNE
Mundi-Prensa Libros S.A.
Castelló 37, Apartado 1223
Madrid 28001   Tel. (91) 431.33.99
                                 Fax: (91) 575.39.98
E-mail: mundiprensa@tsai.es
Internet: http://www.mundiprensa.es

Mundi-Prensa Barcelona
Consell de Cent No. 391
08009 – Barcelona   Tel. (93) 488.34.92
                                 Fax: (93) 487.76.59

Libreria de la Generalitat
Palau Moja
Rambla dels Estudis, 118
08002 – Barcelona
               (Suscripciones) Tel. (93) 318.80.12
               (Publicaciones) Tel. (93) 302.67.23
                               Fax: (93) 412.18.54

SRI LANKA
Centre for Policy Research
c/o Colombo Agencies Ltd.
No. 300-304, Galle Road
Colombo 3   Tel. (1) 574240, 573551-2
                   Fax: (1) 575394, 510711

SWEDEN – SUÈDE
CE Fritzes AB
S–106 47 Stockholm   Tel. (08) 690.90.90
                                 Fax: (08) 20.50.21

For electronic publications only/
Publications électroniques seulement
STATISTICS SWEDEN
Informationsservice
S-115 81 Stockholm   Tel. 8 783 5066
                                 Fax: 8 783 4045

Subscription Agency/Agence d'abonnements :
Wennergren-Williams Info AB
P.O. Box 1305
171 25 Solna   Tel. (08) 705.97.50
                                 Fax: (08) 27.00.71

Liber distribution
Internatinal organizations
Fagerstagatan 21
S-163 52 Spanga

SWITZERLAND – SUISSE
Maditec S.A. (Books and Periodicals/Livres
et périodiques)
Chemin des Palettes 4
Case postale 266
1020 Renens VD 1   Tel. (021) 635.08.65
                                 Fax: (021) 635.07.80

Librairie Payot S.A.
4, place Pépinet
CP 3212
1002 Lausanne   Tel. (021) 320.25.11
                                 Fax: (021) 320.25.14

Librairie Unilivres
6, rue de Candolle
1205 Genève   Tel. (022) 320.26.23
                                 Fax: (022) 329.73.18

Subscription Agency/Agence d'abonnements :
Dynapresse Marketing S.A.
38, avenue Vibert
1227 Carouge   Tel. (022) 308.08.70
                                 Fax: (022) 308.07.99

See also – Voir aussi :
OECD Bonn Centre
August-Bebel-Allee 6
D-53175 Bonn (Germany)   Tel. (0228) 959.120
                                 Fax: (0228) 959.12.17

THAILAND – THAÏLANDE
Suksit Siam Co. Ltd.
113, 115 Fuang Nakhon Rd.
Opp. Wat Rajbopith
Bangkok 10200   Tel. (662) 225.9531/2
                                 Fax: (662) 222.5188

TRINIDAD & TOBAGO, CARIBBEAN TRINITÉ-ET-TOBAGO, CARAÏBES
Systematics Studies Limited
9 Watts Street
Curepe
Trinidad & Tobago, W.I.   Tel. (1809) 645.3475
                                 Fax: (1809) 662.5654
E-mail: tobe@trinidad.net

TUNISIA – TUNISIE
Grande Librairie Spécialisée
Fendri Ali
Avenue Haffouz Imm El-Intilaka
Bloc B 1 Sfax 3000   Tel. (216-4) 296 855
                                 Fax: (216-4) 298.270

TURKEY – TURQUIE
Kültür Yayinlari Is-Türk Ltd.
Atatürk Bulvari No. 191/Kat 13
06684 Kavaklidere/Ankara
                         Tel. (312) 428.11.40 Ext. 2458
                         Fax : (312) 417.24.90
Dolmabahce Cad. No. 29
Besiktas/Istanbul   Tel. (212) 260 7188

UNITED KINGDOM – ROYAUME-UNI
The Stationery Office Ltd.
Postal orders only:
P.O. Box 276, London SW8 5DT
Gen. enquiries   Tel. (171) 873 0011
                                 Fax: (171) 873 8463

The Stationery Office Ltd.
Postal orders only:
49 High Holborn, London WC1V 6HB
Branches at: Belfast, Birmingham, Bristol,
Edinburgh, Manchester

UNITED STATES – ÉTATS-UNIS
OECD Washington Center
2001 L Street N.W., Suite 650
Washington, D.C. 20036-4922 Tel. (202) 785.6323
                                 Fax: (202) 785.0350
Internet: washcont@oecd.org

Subscriptions to OECD periodicals may also be
placed through main subscription agencies.

Les abonnements aux publications périodiques de
l'OCDE peuvent être souscrits auprès des
principales agences d'abonnement.

Orders and inquiries from countries where Distribu-
tors have not yet been appointed should be sent to:
OECD Publications, 2, rue André-Pascal, 75775
Paris Cedex 16, France.

Les commandes provenant de pays où l'OCDE n'a
pas encore désigné de distributeur peuvent être
adressées aux Éditions de l'OCDE, 2, rue André-
Pascal, 75775 Paris Cedex 16, France.

12-1996

OECD PUBLICATIONS, 2, rue André-Pascal, 75775 PARIS CEDEX 16
PRINTED IN FRANCE
(31 97 20 1 P) ISBN 92-64-15491-4 – No. 49453 1997